D1490801

Amped
Published by Orange, a division of The reThink Group, Inc.
5870 Charlotte Lane, Suite 300
Cumming, GA 30040 U.S.A.

The Orange logo is a registered trademark of The reThink Group, Inc.
All rights reserved. Except for brief excerpts for review purposes, no part of this book
may be reproduced or used in any form without written permission from the publisher.

Scripture quotations marked (NIV) are taken from the Holy Bible, New International
Version®, NIV®. Copyright © 1973, 1978, 1984, 2011 by Biblica, Inc.™ Used by
permission of Zondervan. All rights reserved worldwide. www.zondervan.com The
"NIV" and "New International Version" are trademarks registered in the United States
Patent and Trademark Office by Biblica, Inc.™

Scripture quotations marked (NIrV) are taken from the Holy Bible, New International
Reader's Version®, NIrV® Copyright © 1995, 1996, 1998, 2014 by Biblica, Inc.™ Used
by permission of Zondervan. All rights reserved worldwide. www.zondervan.com The
"NIrV" and "New International Reader's Version" are trademarks registered in the
United States Patent and Trademark Office by Biblica, Inc.™

Other Orange products are available online and direct from the publisher. Visit our
website at www.WhatIsOrange.org for more resources like these.

ISBN: 978-1-63570-068-8

©2018 The reThink Group, Inc.

reThink Conceptual Team:

Reggie Joiner, Kristen Ivy, Jon Williams, Mike Clear, Dan Scott, Brandon Odel

Lead Writer: Mike Tiemann

Editing: Lauren Terrell

Project Manager: Nate Brandt

Book Design & Layout: Jacob Hunt

Printed in the United States of America

First Edition 2018
1 2 3 4 5 6 7 8 9 10
03/28/17

**Copies of this book are available for distribution in churches,
schools, and other venues at a significant quantity discount.
For more details, go to www.OrangeStore.org.**

AMPED

LIVE FULLY ALIVE!

START HERE.

I have a quick question for you:

ARE YOU AMPED?

I'm tempted to do that thing where I make you yell "YEAH!" at the top of your lungs over and over by saying things like, "I can't hear you . . . I *said* ARE. YOU. AAAAAAMPED?" Or, *"C'mon, I know you can do better than that!"*

But I won't do that to you . . . because you'd be yelling at a book. Instead, I'll pretend you responded in the most reasonable way:

Shrugging (inside or out) and wondering: *What's there to be amped about? And what does "amped" even mean?*

Let's start with that second question.

Amped (adj.)—fired up, awaiting a big thrill, stoked, ready to roll.

OR

Amped (adj.)—acting as an amplifier; an electronic device that makes something bigger, stronger, LOUDER.

So I guess the question really is:

ARE YOU AMPED TO BE AMPED?

Are you . . .

FIRED UP
STOKED
READY TO GET PLUGGED IN

READY TO **LIVE FULLY ALIVE**?

This is your chance to discover a completely NEW way to live.

Does that sound like too big of a promise?
Well, look at Who said it: **Jesus**.

He said . . .
"I have come so they may have life. I want them to have it in the fullest possible way" **JOHN 10:10b**

Jesus wants "them"—you, me, us, anyone who follows Jesus—to live the fullest life possible. He wants your life to be totally AMPED.

There are two ways to do life:
- You can *exist*.
- Or you can *really live*.

The first way is sort of unavoidable. You breathe in and out. You eat and drink when you need to. You sleep when the sun goes down and wake up each morning.

But the second—*really living*—is a choice that takes confidence. It means really believing what God says is true so you can make not only good choices, but the *best* choices. So you can live fully alive.

So . . . what does God say?
And what are you supposed to do about it?

That's what this book is about.

You only get **one shot** at life.
Are you ready to make the most of it?
Are you ready to make it count?
Are you ready to leave the bunny slopes behind?
Are you ready to shred?
Are you ready to get AMPED?

Okay, okay! Stop shouting at me and start reading.

SUPERCHARGED

1

WEEK 1

SUPERCHARGED

[Hey there! Good to see you again. If you missed the introduction, go back to page 4 and read it first.]

Have you ever seen an extreme athlete in action? Maybe it was a snowboarder, or a BMX freestyler, or a barefoot water-skier. (If the answer is no, pause here and—with an adult's permission—watch a short video on extreme sports. The internet is filled with compilations of extreme athletes doing extreme stunts that make my stomach extremely queasy and my palms extremely sweaty.)

They leap.
They spin.
They flip.
They soar.

It's like they're supercharged.

And while most of us will never understand where these athletes get the skills—or confidence—to attempt these stunts, this week will help you understand how to live a supercharged life; a life that makes eyes pop and jaws drop; a life that's super(naturally) charged by God.

So plug in and find out: Why does Jesus matter?

DAY 1

Jesus matters most.
Ephesians 2:19-21

Every structure is built on something. You can't make a LEGO city without one of those flat, green, grassy pieces underneath it, or the whole thing will crumble. Even structures that seem to be suspended in air—treehouses, bridges, hammocks—are all (hopefully) firmly attached to the ground in some way.

Your life is built on something—or Some*one*—too.

> *"You are citizens together with God's people. You are also members of God's family. You are a building that is built on the apostles and prophets. They are the foundation. Christ Jesus himself is the most important stone in the building. The whole building is held together by him."*
> **EPHESIANS 2:19-21**

Other translations of these verses say Jesus is the "cornerstone." The cornerstone of a building is not just any part of the foundation. It's the very first stone placed in the foundation of a building. All other stones and materials are built off of that one stone.

Like the very first LEGO block you snap into place.

These verses in Ephesians tell us it all started with Jesus. The prophets and apostles who helped spread the word laid the rest of the foundation. And we—anyone who believes Jesus is who He says He is—are all part of this building held together by Jesus. Jesus matters most.

But unlike stones in a builder's hands, you and I get to decide if we want to be a part of this building.

For centuries, many people have believed that Jesus was (and is!) the promised Savior. There are lots of people around you who believe that today. They have all chosen to build their lives on the same thing—Jesus.

But . . . why?

Well, to answer that question, we have to go back a few pages. Remember JOHN 10:10? When Jesus says:

> *I have come so they may have life. I want them to have it in the fullest possible way.*

Everyone who has chosen to build their lives on Jesus, to make Him the cornerstone of their lives, wants to live the fullest possible life.

No, that doesn't mean having the fullest possible calendar. Clubs, sports, vacations, activities, sleepovers, schoolwork, projects . . . I need a nap.

It means living a life bursting with JOY, LOVE, COURAGE, PEACE, ADVENTURE . . . and so much more. It means living fully alive.

We all build our lives on some kind of cornerstone.

. . . our own talents.
. . . our possessions.
. . . our reputations.

But soccer skills fade with time. LEGO collections get scattered by little sisters. And somehow the only way to be happy with who you are is to not really worry about who others think you are.

Jesus, however, never changes, never fades, never breaks. He always sees the very best parts of you. He always wants you to be FULLY ALIVE. Jesus matters most. More than how far you make it in the spelling bee. More than the latest, greatest gaming system. More than what others think of you.

Think about the way you're building YOUR life. Think about what matters most to you. If someone were to look at your life, what would they think matters most to you?

* ///

* ///

* ///

Aren't quite convinced Jesus matters more than your PlayStation? Of course not! It's only the beginning. Come back tomorrow to learn more about what matters most.

DAY 2

You matter.
Matthew 10:29-31

When you first step onto a skateboard, it's hard enough to stay on as it rolls slowly down a hill. But eventually, you learn to keep your balance. Then you learn how to move with the board.

After a while, you get up your nerve to try a trick. A lot of skaters try an ollie first.

Ollie: A trick in skateboarding where the skater kicks the tail of the board down while jumping in order to make the board pop in the air.

In other words, you jump *with* your board. You have to time it just right and push down with your back foot to get the board to "jump" with you.

And what's the first thing a skater does after perfecting their ollie? The same thing a gymnast does after landing their first standing tuck. The same thing a basketball player does after learning to dunk:

"Check this out."
"Look what I can do!"

When you learn something new, you want to show everyone. And it's not just you. It's universal. Everyone does it. Why? Because we want to prove we're worth something. We want to prove we're special, unique, important. We want to *matter*.

And we think the more we know, the more we have, the more we can *do*, the more we matter.

But that's not what God thinks. One day, Jesus told a crowd of people:

> *Aren't two sparrows sold for only a penny? But not one of them falls to the ground outside your Father's care. He even counts every hair on your head! So don't be afraid. You are worth more than many sparrows.*
> **MATTHEW 10:29-31**

Apparently, sparrows (birds) weren't worth more than a penny to the people Jesus was talking to. But God thinks sparrows matter enough for Him to know and orchestrate their every move. Think about how much more YOU matter to Him—whether you can do the sickest ollie or barely stand on a perfectly still board.

God thinks you matter—period!

Remember . . .
God made you.
God loves you.
God has a plan for your life.

He knows exactly how many hairs are on your head. *(The average person has something like 100,000 . . . but only God knows if you've got 93,462 or 154,113.)*

You don't have to do an ollie to get God to notice you. He's already crazy about you! And because you matter so much to God, you can have the confidence to live your fullest life.

How do you think the following parts of your life might change if you *truly believed* you matter, and that you're just as valuable as everyone you know, meet, or see on TV?

How you dress

_____

_____

_____

How you treat others

_____

_____

_____

How you treat yourself

Who you hang out with

mom dad Arell Adv make zoey
Cloe alexa Billie madison ella
Scarlett

DAY 3

Your time matters.
Psalm 90:12 (NIV)

Do you like being a kid? Write down five things that are good about being the age you are right now.

1 _____

2 _____

3 _____

4 _____

5 _____

Are you also kind of ready to be an adult? Write down five things that you think will be cool about being grown-up.

1 //

2 //

3 //

4 //

5 //

When you're a kid, it seems like you have all the time in the world. The year between one birthday and the next feels like an ETERNITY. But this weird thing happens as you get older. Time starts to move faster and faster. One year, you'll feel like you barely had enough time to sweep the birthday confetti off the floor before it's time to celebrate again. (Kinda sounds nice, right?)

But while constant birthday parties and Christmases do have their perks, the older you get, the less and less time you have.

We all have things we want to do in our lives.

Write your name in wet cement.
Solve a Rubik's cube.
Climb a coconut tree barefoot.

But we only have a certain amount of time in our lives. And while time seems to creep along slower than that pet sloth you plan on having one day, it's important to spend that time wisely.

In fact, the only way to live fully alive is to make the best possible choices with our time. Check out **PSALM 90:12 (NIV)**.

> *Teach us to number our days, that we may gain a heart of wisdom.*

"Numbering our days" means making every day count, and seeing each day—each moment—as a gift from God. It means not wasting time on things that don't really matter.

Now is the best time to live like Jesus.
Now is the best time to follow His example.
Now is the best time to grow in your relationship with Him.
Now is the best time to climb a coconut tree barefoot. (You know, if that's your thing.)

Take a minute and think of the top five ways you'd like to spend your time. (I went ahead and filled in the first one for you.) ;)

1 *Reading this devotional*

2

3

4

5

DAY 4

What you believe matters.
Ephesians 2:8-10

This week, we've talked a lot about the things that really matter.

Jesus matters.
You matter.
Your time matters.

But really, none of that makes a difference without what we're talking about today:

What YOU believe.

I'm not talking about whether you believe in ghosts or the Tooth Fairy. Or if you believe the Patriots are the best NFL team of all time (when it's obviously the Steelers). I'm talking about your faith. What you believe about God and who Jesus is.

Here's the truth. God loves you so much that He sent Jesus to Earth over 2,000 years ago. Jesus died on the cross to take the punishment for your sins, and He rose from the dead! If you believe that's true, then you can receive the best gift ever—a relationship with God that will last forever.

Have you ever made the decision to believe and receive God's gift? If not, talk to someone you trust (maybe the person who gave you this book) about what it means to believe that Jesus is your Savior.

If you *have* made that decision, you probably know it's the most important decision you'll EVER make. It's bigger than where you live, what you do for a job, or even who you spend your life with. What you believe matters. It changes . . .

. . . how you treat others.
. . . how you think of yourself.
. . . how you react when something really bad happens.
. . . how you react when something really good happens.
. . . how hard you work.
. . . how hard you play.

What you believe changes everything.

Believing in Jesus is such a huge deal because it's what you were *made* to do. God made you to worship Him and point others to Him. God loves you, and He wants you to be in His family forever!

> God's grace has saved you because of your faith in Christ. Your salvation doesn't come from anything you do. It is God's gift. It is not based on anything you have done. No one can brag about earning it. We are God's creation. He created us to belong to Christ Jesus. Now we can do good works. Long ago God prepared these works for us to do.
> **EPHESIANS 2:8-10**

God sent Jesus to make a way for you to be with God forever. Jesus made it possible for you to have a relationship with God *without* your sin being in the way. He made it possible for you to live a **SUPER**charged life. And it's up to you to decide what you believe—whether or not to be **SUPER**charged.

God wants you to know His love. He wants you to know what it's like to live fully alive—for Him! So sometime in the next day or two, make time to ask a trusted adult—someone you know loves and follows Jesus—this question:

How has what you believe about God changed your life?

DAY 5

Live like Jesus matters most.
John 10:10b

By now you know this book is about learning to live life to its fullest.

Seize the day.
Leave no stone unturned.
Grab the bull by the horns.
Living *la vida loca.*

Anywho . . . like I said on page 5, the idea of living fully alive comes from what Jesus said in John 10:10 (the second part of the verse).

> *I have come so they may have life.*
> *I want them to have it in the fullest possible way.*
> **JOHN 10:10b**

Jesus came to Earth to teach us about who God is, to defeat death, and to make a way for us to be with God—always. He came to give us the fullest possible life. Your Bible might have a different translation with a different word. But they all mean the same thing. Jesus wants us to have a life that's rich, satisfying, and abundant.

Inside this thought bubble, write down some words that come to mind when you think of the *fullest* kind of life:

Maybe you wrote down "exciting" or "adventurous." That's what I think of when I think of living a full life. But I also think of a life that's meaningful—the kind of life that changes me and everyone around me for the better. That's exactly the kind of life Jesus wants for you.

All you have to do is believe Jesus matters most.

When you believe that Jesus matters *most,* you start to live like Jesus matters most. And that's when your life gets supercharged.

You start to forget about the little things.
You find the confidence to tackle the big things.

Living fully alive isn't about what YOU can do.
Living fully alive is about what HE can do . . . through you.

When you live like Jesus matters most, it's a game-changer. It transforms the way you live. Finish out this week by circling the top three things you think would change in your life if you started living like Jesus matters most.

ATTITUDE	CONTENTMENT
FRIENDS	HUMILITY
RELATIONSHIPS	PATIENCE
CONFIDENCE	HONESTY
GRADES	COMPASSION
JOY	SELF-CONTROL
OBEDIENCE	KINDNESS
FAITH	GRATITUDE
DEPENDABILITY	RESPECT
COURAGE	HOPE

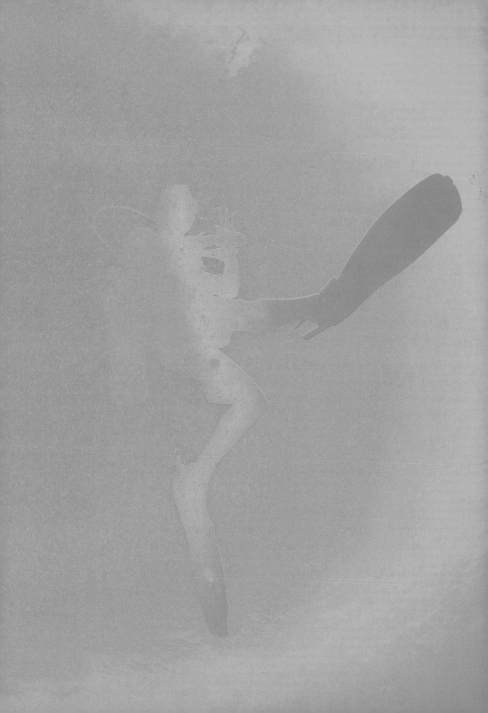

AMP IT UP

By now, you know what matters most: Jesus.

You know that living fully alive means living in a **SUPER**charged way. It means remembering there's a **SUPER**natural side to everything you experience each day. It means remembering your life is connected to something much bigger.

So the question is . . .

How do you stay **SUPER**charged?

How do you remember to *think* that way about life in the middle of actually *living* it?

Believe it or not, the answer is a lot like plugging in a charging cord. You've got to **stay connected**. Your computer, tablet, phone, or other device doesn't do you any good if you forget to keep it charged up.

Try this:

1. Find the charging cord for your tablet, or laptop, or another device that you use a lot in your house.

2. Cut out this tag and wrap it around the charging cord. (Pro tip: Put it close to the part that plugs into your device so you can see it—not the part that plugs into the outlet.)

3. Tape down the folded-over end of the tag so that it stays on the cord.

Every time you plug in that device, it'll remind you to stay connected to God. You can do that by praying, reading your Bible, talking to other people about Him—even taking time each day to read this devotional.

Remember, God is your ultimate power source. He's the reason you can live fully alive. He's the One who can keep you focused on what really matters!

RIDING GOOFY FOOT

3

WEEK 2

Riding Goofy Foot

Cross your arms in front of you. Now try to cross them the other way—with the opposite arm on top.

Interlace your fingers—folding your hands as if you're praying. Now try to fold your hands with the other thumb on top.

Feel a little goofy?

Are you right-handed? Left-handed? (Fun fact: Did you know only about 10% of people in the world are left-handed?)

Did you know your feet have a preference, too? If you're a soccer player, gymnast, skateboarder, snowboarder, wakeboarder (any athlete with a board, really), you know whether you're right-footed or left-footed.

If you're one of those athletes with a board, you know that most people lead with their left foot on the front of the board. But there are a few who naturally lead with their right. This is known as riding goofy foot. (Except for those athletes, it doesn't feel goofy at all.)

God made them to feel more comfortable "riding goofy." And God made you who you are—*on purpose.*

There are so many things that make you, YOU. And some of them might make you feel a little "goofy," or worse: incapable or unworthy. You might be tempted to think "I can't" . . . even when God says, "I can."

You aren't the only one who's felt that way. In fact, the Bible is full of people who thought, "I can't" because they were different or "weird" or had messed up too many times in too many ways.

But God used them anyway to show that when you can't, He can.

How could God use you?

Let's see!

DAY 6

God can use you no matter what.
Judges 6:15-16a

If you've ever been the kid in gym class who can't even do one chin-up, or felt like you're the *only* one in math class who can't seem to wrap your brain around long division . . .

. . . you know how Gideon felt.

Gideon was an Israelite. But not just any Israelite. He was the least important member of the weakest family in the tribe of Manasseh (one of Israel's 12 tribes). So when God put Gideon in charge of defending all of Israel by going to battle against the Midianites, Gideon was sure God had the wrong guy.

And I'm not just being harsh. Gideon said it himself.

> *"How can I possibly save Israel?*
> *My family group is the weakest in the tribe of Manasseh.*
> *And I'm the least important member of my family."*
> **JUDGES 6:15**

See? Whether it was true or not, Gideon thought he was a nobody. But *nobody* is a nobody to God. God can use you no matter what.

Not only did God see Gideon as someone who could defeat a powerful enemy army, God called Gideon a "mighty warrior." He had *chosen* Gideon to lead His army. He told Gideon: *"I will be with you."* JUDGES 6:16

Have you ever felt like Gideon? Have you ever felt like God wanted you to do something you didn't think you could do?

Maybe you think . . .
- I'm not brave enough.
- I'm not smart enough.
- I'm not talented enough.
- I'm not cool enough.
- I'm not strong enough.

It's important to remember what God said to Gideon:

"I will be with you."

Because it's true for you, too. Whether it's standing up to someone (or *for* someone), trying out for the football team or the school play, or sharing what you know about God with someone (or a lot of someones), God can use you. No matter what. And you can have confidence because He is with you.

Use the space below to write two words: "I CAN'T."

Now scratch through "I CAN'T" and write: "HE CAN."

It's not about having everything together. It's not about trying to be someone you're not.

It's about trust. Trusting that God is with you. Trusting that He can use you. *Knowing* that He can help you to do anything He's asked you to do.

DAY 7

God can see the real you.
1 Samuel 16:7

Today's going to look a little different. Take this book to your bathroom sink and read it in the mirror.

God sees the things that are hidden away. He sees the reasons why you do what you do. A mirror can show you what's on the outside. But **God can see the real you**—inside and out.

Take at least five minutes to close your eyes and ask God these questions.

- What am I really good at?
- How would You like to use me to make a difference in the world around me?
- What is holding me back from doing what You've asked me to do?

Now sit in silence and listen to God—to the One who sees the real you. (Note: Listening to God is different from listening to your friends and family. God is inside you and He speaks in all kinds of ways. Whether it's a booming, eardrum-bursting voice or an exciting idea that makes your heart swell or your stomach churn, let God work in your thoughts and lead your heart.)

What did you learn? Did you hear or feel God in any way? Do you have any guesses on how God would answer those questions for you? Write those thoughts out on the next couple of pages . . .

Good, you made it!  **START HERE!**

Here's a question. **Who knows the real you?**

Your parents?
Your siblings?
Your best friends?

They all know you really well. But they still don't know everything about you. The only One who knows ALL about you . . .

. . . is GOD!

God knows you better than you know yourself. (Mind . . . blown!) He sees things that YOU don't even see. He sees why you make decisions. He understands your hopes and dreams, your struggles and disappointments, and the things that give you the greatest joy.

You see, God isn't really concerned with what's on the surface. He cares most about what's in your heart.

If you ever wonder if that's true, look at the life of David. David was an unlikely choice to be the king of Israel. When the prophet Samuel came to town to choose the new king, everyone was sure Samuel would pick one of David's older brothers.

In fact, even Samuel figured that David's older brother Eliab would be the one God had chosen. After all, Eliab was tall and handsome. He looked like a king. But check out what God told Samuel:

"The Lord does not look at the things people look at. People look at the outside of a person. But the Lord looks at what is in the heart."
1 SAMUEL 16:7

DAY 8

God can see your potential.
Exodus 4:11-12

You may have seen drawings like these in your science textbook. Or heard the terms "potential energy" and "kinetic energy" in class. And while they're big words and may have been explained in a very confusing way, "potential" and "kinetic" are pretty simple.

potential: what something *could* do
kinetic: what something *is* doing

POTENTIAL

KINETIC

YOU have potential, like a rock pulled back in a slingshot. But, unlike that rock, it's sometimes hard to know *what* your potential is.

The rock in the slingshot is going to fly wherever the slingshot is aimed. The ball at the top of the hill is going to roll down the slope. The lightbulb is going to light up when the electricity flows freely.

But what are *you* going to do? What potential do *you* have?

One of the first main characters in God's BIG story wondered the same thing. He'd already had a pretty incredible life: born to a family of Israelite slaves in Egypt, hidden in a basket as a baby so he wouldn't be killed, found by a princess and raised in a palace, exiled to the desert for killing an Egyptian who was beating an Israelite slave.

To Moses, and anyone who knew Moses, it seemed his potential had vanished. He'd completed the thrilling, "kinetic" part of his life—and all that was left was watching sheep in the middle of nowhere.

But God could see Moses's potential.

One day, God appeared to Moses in a burning bush. He told Moses: *"I want you to bring the Israelites out of Egypt. They are my people."* EXODUS 3:10

At first, Moses wasn't so sure about God's plan. He couldn't see his potential to lead anyone. He didn't know how to give speeches that would . . .

. . . rally a generation of Israelites to revolt.

. . . convince a power-hungry Pharaoh to let about a million of his slaves to go free.

. . . give courage, strength, and confidence to God's abused and overlooked people.

But God knew all this. God made Moses. He knew his past. He knew his present. He knew his potential. God *knew* that Moses wasn't the greatest speaker. And God chose Moses to lead His people anyway!

Look at God's reply:

> "Who makes human beings able to talk? Who makes them unable to hear or speak? Who makes them able to see? Who makes them blind? It is I, the Lord. Now go. I will help you speak. I will teach you what to say."
> **EXODUS 4:11-12**

God can see your potential, too.

God made you. He knows what you've done. He knows your past. But more importantly, He knows your potential. And it may surprise you. In fact, it's almost guaranteed to surprise you. You may think your life is standing on flat ground, seeing nothing but flat land for miles in every direction. But God can see the loaded spring beneath you, ready to toss you higher than you ever thought you could go.

The question is: Will you have the confidence to trust God's plan? Or will you flail wildly and scream, "Who put that spring theerrrre?!" when your potential becomes kinetic?

DAY 9

God can use you even when you mess up.
Luke 19:8

Time for a pop quiz! Answer quickly and write your answers here on the page.

- What do cows drink?
- There are five horses, but two fall asleep. How many are still standing?
- Which is heavier—a pound of feathers or a pound of gold?

You'd think the answers would be milk, three horses, and gold.

Actually, cows drink water . . . it's five horses (they sleep standing up) . . . and both the feathers and the gold weigh the same (a pound is a pound).

If you got those wrong, don't worry. Everyone does. (And now you can use them to trick your friends—ha!)

Everyone messes up. Sometimes it's not that big of a deal, like missing a question on a pop quiz. But sometimes it's a bigger deal, like lying to your parents or saying something mean to a friend.

The good news is, God will *always* forgive you. It doesn't matter if it's something big or something small. You can always talk to God and tell Him about it. He loves you! He'll give you a fresh start. He can even help you make a different choice next time.

There's a funny thing that can happen with mess-ups, though. Even when God forgives you, you might still *feel* badly about what you did. You might even feel like the things you've done wrong in the past will keep you from being able to do good things in the future.

Look at what happened with Zacchaeus. (You can read his story in Luke 19.) When Jesus came to Jericho, the people in town all wanted to have a meal with Him. But Jesus went to Zacchaeus' house even though Zacchaeus was known to be a cheater and a thief. Why would Jesus hang out with someone like *that?* Even Zacchaeus himself was shocked.

But what the people of Jericho learned that day—Zacchaeus included—was this: God can use you even when you mess up.

Jesus loved Zacchaeus just like He loves you. He didn't disqualify Zacchaeus just because he had done wrong things in the past. And Zacchaeus was so amazed by the way Jesus loved him that he said:

> *"Look, Lord! Here and now I give half of what I own to those who are poor. And if I have cheated anybody out of anything, I will pay it back. I will pay back four times the amount I took."*
> **LUKE 19:8**

Zacchaeus didn't let his mess-ups get in the way of the good he could do right then and there.

What good can *you* do right now? Ask for forgiveness for your mess-ups—and then leave them behind, so you can live fully alive!

DAY 10

God can use you right now.
1 Timothy 4:12

Match the accomplishment in column A to the age of the youngest person to achieve it in column B. (No computers, tablets, or smartphones!)

Youngest person to . . .

Graduate college	10
Climb Mount Everest	19
Win a Grammy	11
Compete in the Olympics	14
Program a video game	12
Become a billionaire	13
Become a New York Times bestselling author	7

Do you ever feel like people don't give you a chance because you're young? Maybe you've felt like you're too young to really make a difference. The truth is, God can use you right now!

That's what Paul told his friend Timothy. Timothy and Paul were working together to share the good news about Jesus. Timothy looked up to Paul, and Paul encouraged him along the way to live out what he believed.

We know all of this from reading the stories and letters in the New Testament. We also know that Paul wanted Timothy to feel confident in his faith, even though he was young.

Paul told him:

> *Don't let anyone look down on you because you are young. Set an example for the believers in what you say and in how you live. Also set an example in how you love and in what you believe.*
> **1 TIMOTHY 4:12**

Underline the part where Paul wrote, "set an example." You can do that right now—no waiting!

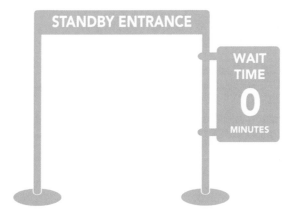

When you make the wise choice . . .
when you trust God no matter what . . .
when you treat others the way you want to be treated . . .
other people notice!

They can see how God is making a difference in your life by the way you're living—*fully alive.*

author (12)
Become a billionaire (19), Become a New York Times bestselling
(14), Compete in the Olympics (10), Program a video game (7),
Graduate college (11), Climb Mount Everest (13), Win a Grammy
ANSWERS

It can be so simple!
You can listen to a friend who's having a bad day.
You can let your little brother choose the pizza toppings.
You can make a card to thank your mail carrier.

You don't need to wait around until you finish college.
You don't need to be an "expert" in anything.
It's not even about what *you* can do in the first place.

It's about what *God* can do through you.
Living fully alive is about the choices you make—the way you live your life.
And you can make those choices today. You can live what you believe *right now*!

AMP IT UP

Let's have some fun . . . "goofy foot" style!

If you have a skateboard or scooter, try "riding switch." In other words, ride goofy if you normally ride regular, or ride regular if you normally ride goofy. (Don't forget your helmet and pads!)

If you have a wiffle ball set, ask someone to pitch to you and try batting the opposite way.

Try to kick a soccer ball with your opposite foot.

How about some more everyday things? Try these with your opposite hand.
- Brush your teeth.
- Brush your hair.
- Write your name.
- Use a fork or spoon to eat something.

What happened when you tried to switch it up? You probably weren't as successful, right? You probably thought . . .

"I can't do this."

We tell ourselves that a lot in life. We think we can't do the things God wants us to do. We forget that He's right there with us—that His power is working in us.

God made you who you are for a reason. Even if you feel like you're not _____ enough (fill in the blank), never forget that God can use you.

He can use you no matter what.
He can see the real you.
He can see your potential.
He can use you even when you mess up.
He can use you right now.

Regular or goofy . . . whichever way you ride in life . . . ride *fully alive*!

THE ANCHOR

3

WEEK 3

The Anchor

There are a couple of different ways to go up El Capitan in Yosemite. Some people are perfectly happy to hike a trail around the back. But the real thrill-seekers like to climb straight up the cliff face.

It looks something like this.

El Capitan is about 3,000 feet straight up, so it usually takes multiple days to get to the top. That means you have to sleep on a ledge on the side of the cliff. Can you imagine?

If you're halfway up a mountain, you definitely need to be able to trust your ropes. They need to be hooked to something secure. In the climbing world, it's called an anchor.

A climbing anchor isn't like the kind that you'd see on a ship. It's actually a system of "anchor points" that are either part of the rock, or gear that you place in the rock. You connect the points together and then clip into them.

The goal is simple: to keep you anchored on that mountain, even if your hands or feet slip!

Where are you setting *your* anchor? What's anchoring your life? What gives you strength? What keeps you from falling?

If you're not careful, you could anchor yourself to things, or people, instead of God. You might even be tempted to "free-solo" your life and try to climb without any safety ropes at all. (Not a good idea. At all.)

It's worth asking the question . . .
What happens when you trust yourself more than God?

DAY 11

God is stronger than anyone.
Judges 16:28

If you could have one superpower, what would it be?

_____

_____

Samson's story is pretty wild. Even before he was born, he was set apart to lead God's people. His whole life was supposed to be about following God's path.

God even gave Samson a superpower: superhuman strength . . . as long as he never cut his hair. Unfortunately, he told the woman he loved, Delilah, the secret of his strength—and (surprise!) Delilah gave his secret away to his enemy: the Philistines. While Samson was sleeping one night, the Philistines snuck in to cut his hair and tie him up.

When Samson woke up, he was still pretty sure of himself. He thought he could easily break the ropes around him:

> *"I'll go out just as I did before. I'll shake myself free."*
> **JUDGES 16:20**

But, of course, his strength was gone.

Later, Samson remembered where his strength *really* came from. This time, he prayed to God to help him fight the Philistines:

> "Lord and King, show me that you still have concern for me. Please, God, make me strong just one more time."
> **JUDGES 16:28**

And this time, God gave Samson the strength to break his bonds and destroy the Philistine temple, and all the Philistines in it, in one blow.

There's a big difference in those two statements Samson made, isn't there? In the first one, Samson figured he could do it himself. He relied on his own strength to get him through any battle. But then he learned the hard way that he really depended on God for everything.

God is stronger than anyone. He's given each of us gifts, talents, and abilities . . . but it's important not to get so wrapped up in our own abilities that we anchor ourselves in them instead of God. We need to keep in mind where our strength really comes from to begin with: from our relationship with God.

Write down a phrase for each letter that reminds you of how God gives you strength. I'll get you started.

S *tays by my side*

T

R

O

N

G

DAY 12

No one protects you like God.
Psalm 28:7

What does a shield do?

Shields protect soldiers or warriors. And as Captain America has taught us all, shields also *look* cool. In medieval times, they were often decorated with designs and symbols that reminded everyone who the soldiers were fighting for—kind of like how skaters today decorate their boards with stickers and symbols. Usually, those designs mean something important to them.

Here's a shield you can decorate. It has nine sections for you to add in the nine symbols for each chapter of this book. For example, the first one is the lightning bolt from Week 1 (Supercharged).

See if you can draw in the goofy foot symbol from last week and the anchor symbol from this week. You can keep adding the other symbols to your shield as you complete the sections of this book. Eventually, you'll have a cool reminder of what it looks like to live fully alive!

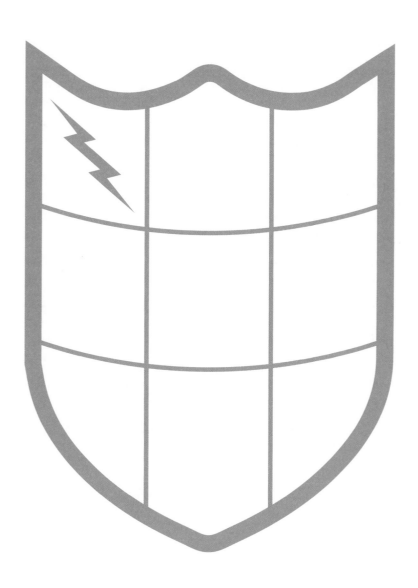

In **PSALM 28:7**, David says this:

> *The Lord gives me strength. He is like a shield that keeps me safe. My heart trusts in him, and he helps me.*
> **PSALM 28:7**

God is like a shield. Have you ever heard that? God is like the biggest, strongest, solidest shield. He has the power to protect you and keep you safe.

Still, sometimes things happen that are confusing or scary. Sometimes things happen that *hurt*. And when those things happen, it's hard to trust that the great, big shield of your relationship with God did much good at all. In those times, it's important to remember that while we can't see the whole picture of how God is working in our lives and in the world, we *can* know that He loves us deeply and that He'll never leave our side.

Like the biggest shield you can imagine, you can trust that God is able to protect you. After all, He's God. And even though He never promises a pain-free life, **no one protects you like God.**

P.S. If it seems like that great, big shield of God has failed and someone or something has hurt you, tell a trusted adult (a coach, teacher, parent, aunt, older sibling, friend's parent, etc.). Sometimes these people can make up God's shield of protection. He has put them in your life for a reason. (And keep reading.)

DAY 13

No one guides you like God.
Psalm 119:105

Do you have a flashlight in your house? Or even better, a headlamp? If you do, use it to read today's devotional.

Even in the most extreme sports, you don't just point your wheels and roll. You've got to do some prep work first. You've got to know where you're going.

You wouldn't climb a mountain without first scouting out the route—the handholds and ledges and cracks you could use along the way.

You wouldn't go whitewater rafting down a raging river if you didn't know anything about the rapids ahead.

You wouldn't skydive out of an airplane without a really good plan about where you're going to land.

If you try to just "wing it" and figure it out as you go, you probably won't be successful. That's how people end up needing to be rescued from the side of a mountain!

In life, you can *try* to go at it alone . . . but that's not the way it was meant to be. That's not how God designed it. God designed you, me, all of us, to be constantly connected to Him because HE knows the handholds and ledges. HE knows what lies ahead. HE knows the plan.

You can't see what's ahead of you the way your Creator can. Which is why **no one guides you like God.**

Read **PSALM 119:105**:

> *Your word is like a lamp that shows me the way.*
> *It is like a light that guides me.*

When you feel lost and you can't quite see the right path to take, God's Word—the Bible—is like a bright light. It's full of wisdom and stories of how God has worked in the lives of people for thousands of years. It can help show you where God wants *you* to go, too.

Sometimes the way ahead might be tough to see. Sometimes you might feel like plunging ahead in the darkness without stopping to turn on the light—to check in with God. But don't forget to read God's words to you. They'll lead you where you really need to go. **Remember: No one guides you like God.**

P.S. If you'd like to read God's Word but don't know where to start, check out these books of the Bible: Matthew, Mark, Proverbs, and Psalms.

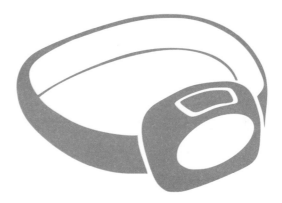

DAY 14

No one cares for you like God.
Psalm 23:1

If you've had any doubts that extreme sports have anything to do with the Bible, check out this verse by David (the shepherd):

> Sometimes a lion or a bear would come and carry off a sheep from the flock. Then I would go after it and hit it. I would save the sheep it was carrying in its mouth. If it turned around to attack me, I would grab its hair.
> **1 SAMUEL 17:34-35**

I don't know about you, but I think if I were given the choice between snowboarding and fighting off a lion with my bare hands . . . I'd hit the slopes every time.

David was a pretty extreme guy. He was a king, a warrior, and perhaps *most extreme*: a shepherd. So when he wrote:

> The Lord is my shepherd. He gives me everything I need.
> **PSALM 23:1**

David knew what a shepherd's job was really like. He knew herding sheep was insanely hard work. David knew it meant . . .
. . . tirelessly chasing down one stray sheep.
. . . gently guiding unwilling flocks across rough terrain to find better land.
. . . and protecting your livestock from predators (like lions and bears).

When David said God was his "shepherd," he meant God was his Rescuer, his Encourager, his Protector, his Gentle Guide, and Fierce Fighter. David meant that God cares for us all like a shepherd cares for his flock.

God cares for *you* the same way. He gives you everything you need. He pursues you when you wander. He walks with you through rough patches and leads you to better days. He protects you with the ferocity of a man fighting a lion barehanded.

Take a moment to draw an image of (or an image that reminds you of) an extreme shepherd:

No one cares for you like God. You can live confidently because you know how much He loves you. He'd go up against lions or bears for you—any day!

DAY 15

No one helps you like God.
Psalm 121:1-3

How many _____ before you got tired?

. . . miles could you run . . .   _____

. . . burpees could you do . . .   _____

. . . movies could you watch . . .   _____

. . . pages could you read . . .   _____

. . . laps could you swim . . .   _____

No matter how strong you are . . . eventually, you'd get tired.

Surfing looks like so much fun when the surfer is riding a monster wave. But you rarely get to see all the kicking and paddling it takes to get into position. Can you say exhausting?

An Olympic triathlete can swim a *mile*, bike 25 miles, and THEN run 6.2 miles—usually in under two hours. Now *that* takes some training.

In 2010 at Wimbledon, two tennis players competed in a single match that lasted 11 hours. Their legs probably felt like Jell-O!

In 1984, two chess players began a chess match that spanned 48 games over *five months*. It finally had to be called off because one of the players had lost over 20 pounds over the course of the match.

All of us get tired. All of us hit a wall. All of us need help in life.

Sometimes you don't want to admit it. You get too bogged down with your responsibilities. There's homework and chores and piano and friendships. There are sleepovers and sports and clubs and parents. And you're *wiped out* . . . but somehow everyone around you seems to be juggling it all easily.

Sometimes you can't help but admit it. Life can throw fastballs, one after the other. There are arguments and divorce and custody and moving. There's sickness and death and funerals. There's job loss and anger and poverty and addiction. And while no one, no matter their age, could juggle that stuff easily, you're just a kid. And you're *done*.

So what do you do?

> I look up to the mountains. Where does my help come from? My help comes from the Lord. He is the Maker of heaven and earth. He won't let your foot slip. He who watches over you won't get tired.
> **PSALM 121:1-3**

God is your anchor. When you need help . . . when you're tired . . . you can put ALL your trust in Him and know He never gets tired. He is always with you.

He can help you . . .

- Finish what you've started, even when you're tired and want to quit.
- Make the wise choice, even when others around you are doing something unwise.
- Have peace and hope when bad things happen along the way.

Life can get busy. It can get full. It can get heavy. It can get exhausting. Don't keep your exhaustion inside.

Turn to God. Talk to Him. He's always with you . . . and **no one helps you like God**.

AMP IT UP

Sometimes life is an easy stroll. Other times it's like you're climbing straight up a cliff face . . . without an anchor or rope.

That's when you *really* find out where your strength comes from. If you're counting on your own strength to get you through, it may run out. But when God is your anchor, He holds you up. You can rely on His power.

He's strong when you're weak.
He protects you like a shield.
He guides you like a lamp.
He cares for you like a shepherd.
He helps you. He won't let your foot slip. He'll never grow tired.

Let's do some creative climbing around your house, shall we?

First, you'll need to find your climbers. They can be action figures . . . stuffed animals . . . even LEGO people. (Probably not your cat, though.)

Now find a good anchor point. It needs to be something strong and secure. It could be the bannister at the top of the stairs, a nail stuck in the top of a door frame (ask your parents first!), or the rails of a bunk bed.

Now you need to connect your climbers together. There are lots of different materials you could use to do this. Yarn, rubber bands, tape, zip ties, cloth napkins, scarves, swimming rings . . . use your imagination!

Start at the top by connecting your lead climber to the anchor. Then connect the other climbers, one by one. How many can you rope together?

Your family will probably be wondering what in the world you're up to. Just tell them you've got some climbers who need a really strong anchor to hold them up!

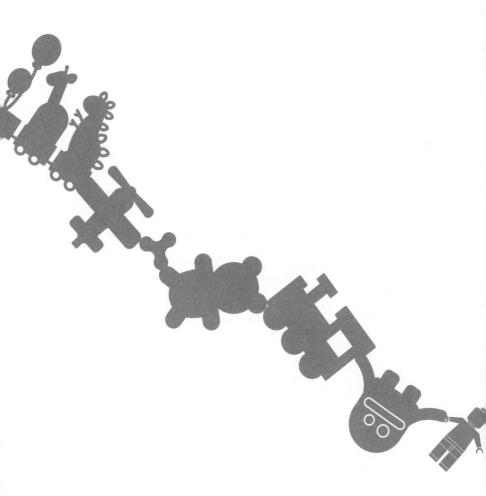

IMPOSSIBLE IS NOTHING

4

WEEK 4

Impossible Is Nothing

When you're learning to ride a bike, it seems impossible.

You try to balance, but you keep leaning from side to side. Luckily, the training wheels are there to catch you. But the only way to *really* learn is to try it without them. You need to get some speed up . . . pedal . . . and trust!

Your first few rides won't be perfect. You'll probably have skinned knees and palms for a little while. But eventually, you'll get it. You'll learn to stay balanced.

Pedaling down the street is one thing. But have you seen what BMX and motocross riders can do? Talk about impossible!

Not to take away from your amazing accomplishment of learning to ride a two-wheeler, but pro athletes can do things the rest of us can barely imagine. Musicians, too—and artists. We're in awe of anyone who can do the seemingly impossible.

They can do it because they have talent (and lots and lots of hours of practice under their belts). But God can do things that really *should* be impossible.

Turn a stick into a snake.
Set fire to a soaking wet altar.
Feed thousands of people with five loaves of bread and two fish.

God can do those things . . . because He's God!

Nothing is impossible for Him.
Do you believe that?

How would you live if you believed God could do the impossible?

DAY 16

God can do the impossible.
1 Kings 18:33-39

Let's play "Possible or Impossible." Put the letter "P" in the blank next to statements that seem possible. Put the letter "I" next to statements that seem impossible.

_____ Ice is made from glass.
_____ A piece of square paper can be folded in half 50 times.
_____ Some people can curl their tongues.
_____ If you look in someone's right ear, you can see through to their left.
_____ There are more stars in the universe than anyone can count in a lifetime.

You know who *really* believed God could do the impossible? A guy named Elijah.

Elijah was a prophet, which meant that God spoke to His people through Elijah. Elijah would listen to God and tell the people what God wanted to tell them.

One day, God had a message for King Ahab—who was the king of Israel at the time—and it wasn't good.

Ahab had been following other gods and encouraging the rest of the people to worship them too. So Elijah was sent to set the record straight and make sure the people knew about the one and only REAL God. Elijah told Ahab to gather all his prophets of the false gods and tell all the Israelites to meet on Mount Carmel.

It was an epic showdown. Elijah gave the people a chance to decide what they really believed. Would they worship Ahab's false gods? Or the one true God?

God told Elijah to have both sides prepare a sacrifice, then pray and see whichever "god" answered by sending down fire from above. Ahab's prophets went first. They prayed to their false gods for hours and hours . . . but of course, nothing happened. Then it was Elijah's turn.

> *"Fill four large jars with water," he said. "Pour it on the offering and the wood. . . . Do it again. . . . Do it a third time."*
> **1 KINGS 18:33-34**

Whoa. Elijah was fully expecting God to bring down the inferno—to do something that only God could do. And he was so absolutely confident in God that he asked the people to SOAK the wood with water, *three times*. There was NO way Elijah could have started a fire after that . . . only God could. Only God can do the impossible.

Sure enough, God sent fire down, and burned up everything on the altar. The fire even dried up all the water that had poured down into the ditch. The people saw it with their own eyes and exclaimed:

"The Lord is the one and only God! The Lord is the one and only God!" **1 KINGS 18:39**

But it came as no surprise to Elijah because he knew that **God can do the impossible.**

Maybe you're thinking, "Yeah, if God were speaking to me like He spoke to Elijah, I might have that confidence, too." But did you know that God wants to speak to you like He spoke to Elijah? God wants you to know Him so well that you're as confident in Him as Elijah was.

Maybe you're not there yet. And that's okay! Your confidence in God can grow. That's one of the reasons why God has preserved His Word for us for thousands and thousands of years. So we could read about His miracles, His love, His strength. So we could learn about who He is and what He can do. So we can learn to listen to Him and see Him in action . . . and be just as confident in His power as Elijah was.

How would your life look different if you truly believed God could do the impossible?

DAY 17

God can make something from nothing.
Jeremiah 32:17

Write down your favorite recipe. (It could be something super-simple, like how to make yourself a bowl of cereal.)

_____

_____

_____

_____

_____

_____

Whether you're applying to Master Chef Junior next month or you can barely toast bread, you know how to make *something*.

But did you know God can (and did) make *everything* from . . . wait for it . . . *nothing?*

He already did! In the beginning, God created the heavens and the earth. He said, *"Let there be light" (Genesis 1:3),* and there was light. He made the sky, the land, and the sea. He made plants. He made the sun, moon, and stars. He made fish . . . birds . . . animals . . . and people. No recipe. No ingredients. No instructions.

What's your favorite animal?

Guess what? God made it! He thought it up out of nowhere and made it out of nothing.

The prophet Jeremiah knew what God could do.
Listen to his prayer:

> *"Lord and King, you have reached out your great and powerful arm. You have made the heavens and the earth. Nothing is too hard for you."*
> **JEREMIAH 32:17**

No matter what you're facing, what you're in the middle of, or what you've just been through, God is right there with you.

Nothing is . . .

too scary
too messy
too bad
too ugly
too painful

. . . for God.

No matter what, you can be sure that **God can make something from nothing**. And He will be with you through everything.

DAY 18

God can bring you out of trouble.
Exodus 14:21-22

Remember how God appeared to Moses in a burning bush? We talked about that back on Day 8. God wanted Moses to lead His people out of Egypt (where they were enslaved). God knew Moses could do it, with His help.

And Moses did! But as God's people were fleeing Egypt, they ran into some trouble. There was literally an ocean standing in their way—the Red Sea.

Pharaoh and his soldiers had chased Moses and the Israelites all the way to the sea. There was nowhere else they could go. They were trapped!

But Moses wasn't worried. Moses knew God could bring them out of trouble. *"Don't be afraid,"* he said. *"Stand firm. You will see how the L*ORD *will save you today."* **EXODUS 14:13**

Moses reached out his hand over the sea, and God divided the waters with a strong wind. The Israelites went through the sea on dry ground, with a wall of water on each side!

Impossible, right? Not for God.

He knows you find yourself in sticky situations sometimes, too. Somebody might say something mean to you on the playground. You might not be getting along well with a friend or family member. You might be anxious about what's going to happen in the future.

God can bring you out of trouble. God is powerful enough to give you a way through those troubles, just like He did for Moses and the Israelites.

One thing God gives us in those times are important relationships with other people—people who love Him and follow Him. Those people can help you remember what's true. They can encourage you when you feel trapped and alone. They might point you toward a solution to your problem. They might remind you how God is with you in the midst of your troubles. Either way, they can help you to be strong and confident in the middle of whatever you're facing.

Who are three people you trust who love and follow God?

1. _____

2. _____

3. _____

DAY 19

God can help you stand for what's right.
Daniel 6:19-22

Have you ever been face-to-face with a lion? Probably not.

Let's be honest. If you've even seen a lion at the zoo, you probably saw a blob of golden, snoring fur.

Maybe you've been lucky enough to see one standing on the rocks, roaring like Mufasa . . . but they don't usually do that during the heat of the day. So it's hard for us to imagine just how scary a real lion encounter would be.

Daniel had his own version of an "extreme lion encounter." He ended up spending a night surrounded by some big, hungry cats—not because he had done something wrong, but because he *kept* doing what was right.

Yep. You read that right. Back when (and where) Daniel lived, you could get in trouble—like eaten-by-lions trouble—for doing the *right* thing (in God's eyes).

Darius, the King of Babylon, had chosen Daniel to be one of three important leaders of his kingdom. Daniel did such a great job that the king wanted to put him in charge of *everything*—which made the other leaders extremely jealous.

These guys tried to come up with a way to take Daniel down. They knew Daniel believed in God, so they told the king:

> *"Don't let any of your people pray to any god or human being except to you. If they do, throw them into the lions' den."*
> **DANIEL 6:7**

See what they did there? Pretty sneaky, huh?

Still, that didn't stop Daniel from doing the right thing. It didn't stop him from talking to God like he had always done. Sure enough, some officials saw him praying, and told King Darius. Darius felt like he had no choice but to follow the law . . . and throw Daniel to the lions!

Picture it: alone . . . in a cold, dark cave, sealed up from the outside world, filled with hungry, man-eating LIONS!

Daniel didn't stand a chance.

But God did the impossible! The next morning, Daniel reported to the king that God had sent an angel—and the angel SHUT the mouths of the lions.

You can stand for what's right, like Daniel did. You won't know for sure what the outcome will be. But you DO know that God will be with you . . . and **He can help you stand for what's right.**

DAY 20

God can do more than you can imagine.
Ephesians 3:20

The escape room phenomenon has hit . . . hard. In just a few years, the world went from never having heard of an escape room to having thousands of different escape room locations to choose from worldwide. From London to Honolulu, Tokyo to Dubai, people are paying anywhere from $4 to $40 to get locked in a room with seemingly no way out.

(And if you haven't done one, I highly suggest it as your next family game night.)

While escape rooms are a great source of entertainment, getting (or feeling) trapped in real life is an entirely different story. When we're stuck—emotionally, physically, situationally—when we can't imagine a way out of whatever trouble we're in, we get discouraged, frantic, desperate.

The good news is, God doesn't. He is calm, cool, and collected because there are endless possibilities for the God of the universe. You may not be able to imagine a way out, but **God can do more than you can imagine.**

Take a minute to write down a situation you're in (or have been in) that seems impossible:

_____

_____

_____

_____

_____

_____

_____

_____

Now, check out this verse:

> *God is able to do far more than we could ever ask for or imagine. He does everything by his power that is working in us.*
> **EPHESIANS 3:20**

How does that verse make you feel? Do you believe it? Why or why not?

_____

_____

_____

_____

_____

_____

_____

_____

We can't even imagine what God is capable of. He's infinitely creative. His wisdom, strength, and power are beyond anything we can understand.

The best part is, God wants you know to know Him personally. He wants you to share your deepest thoughts and feelings with Him. You don't have to hold back because He knows you better than anyone!

Talk to Him. Tell Him how you feel. Tell Him your hopes and dreams. Tell Him your struggles. Let Him guide you.

You might not see a way out right now. But there's always more to the story. **And your God CAN do more than you can imagine!**

AMP IT UP

Let's see if you can make some "impossible shots!"

(If you can, watch "Extreme Trick Shots" by Dude Perfect first.)

Do you have any ping pong balls around your house?
How about wiffle balls?
You need at least five of them.
If not, you can crumple up a few pieces of paper. Those will work, too.

Now you need a bucket . . . or a big, tall mixing bowl.

You'll also need two cloth napkins.

Take all the supplies outside if you can. It could be your backyard or the neighborhood park. (Your mom will be so glad you're getting some fresh air.)

Oh—and grab a friend, a brother, or a sister.

This game is pretty simple to understand—and it's fun, too! But it's *not* easy. Here's how you play:
- Set the bucket on the ground.
- Walk 10 steps away from it.
- Tie a napkin around your head, as a blindfold.
- See how many ping pong balls (real ones or paper ones) you can throw into the bucket.
- Before you throw, say, "Impossible is nothing!" (It's more fun that way.)
- Your friend will keep score for you and cheer you on.

The next time around, try it from 12 steps away. You can keep adding steps to make it more challenging.

See how many "impossible shots" you can get. And remember, nothing is impossible for God!

DROPPING IN

5

WEEK 5

Dropping In

"Dropping in" takes some serious guts!

That's how you get from the edge of a ramp down into the half pipe. It's straight up and down, with no turning back—so a lot of beginner skaters take their time before trying it. They stay on the sidewalk . . . or they might climb down to the bottom of the ramp, so they can start from a safe, flat surface.

It can be pretty scary the first time you go vertical—the first time you drop in.

First, you "set your tail." You lay the flat back part of the board snug over the edge of the ramp, while the rest of your board hangs out over the drop-off. Then you stomp your front foot down onto your board, lean into it, and GO!

Trusting God takes courage, too. Sometimes it can feel like dropping into a half pipe.

But at some point, you've got to go for it. You've got to put yourself out there and trust. You've got to **drop in**.

So . . . **what does it mean to trust God?**
Set your tail because that's what this week is all about. Get ready to drop in!

DAY 21

Trust that God is always with you.
Daniel 3:16-18

What IS trust, anyway?

It's believing.
It's being 100% SURE of something.
It's like putting all your weight on a skateboard that's hanging over the edge of a half pipe.

You're trusting that the wheels won't fall off.
You're trusting that your arms will help you balance.
You're trusting that your helmet and pads will keep you from getting too hurt.

We put our trust in things—and people—all the time. When life goes the way we expect it to . . . when people come through the way we think they will . . . we feel confident and courageous.

But that confidence doesn't *always* come so easily, does it?

The world isn't perfect. Sometimes people let you down. Sometimes what you *thought* would happen . . . doesn't.

Take a minute and think about the last time someone let you down or something unexpected happened. Maybe it was something that *didn't* happen, and it left you feeling unsure about who you could trust.

Go ahead . . . I'll wait.

I can't read your thoughts, but everyone knows what it's like to be let down—and how hard it can be to trust again after that happens.

That's why it's so important to know that you can ALWAYS trust God. You can trust Him no matter what! He is always with you. When your life is going great, AND when things are a bit of a mess, God never changes. He always loves you. He's always there to give you the strength you need to get up, dust yourself off, and keep going.

Have you ever heard of Shadrach, Meshach, and Abednego? These three friends trusted God in a pretty BIG way. They refused to bow down and worship a golden statue that the king had made. The king had *commanded* everyone to worship it . . . or else he'd throw them in a fiery furnace!

Listen to what these three guys said to the king. Can you see where *their* courage came from?

> *"We might be thrown into the blazing furnace. But the God we serve is able to bring us out of it alive. He will save us from your power. But we want you to know this, Your Majesty. Even if we knew that our God wouldn't save us, we still wouldn't serve your gods. We wouldn't worship the gold statue you set up."*
> **DANIEL 3:17-18**

Shadrach, Meshach, and Abednego *trusted* that God was with them—whether He saved them or not. And God did save them—they came out of the furnace completely unharmed! Even though they were in a scary situation, they knew the secret of real courage: **trusting that God is always with you**.

Sometimes God keeps you from harm. Sometimes God is simply with you through the pain. But God is ALWAYS with you. How does it help to know He's there no matter what?

DAY 22

Don't be afraid because God is always with you.
Isaiah 41:10

> "Do not be afraid. I am with you.
> Do not be terrified. I am your God.
> I will make you strong and help you.
> I will hold you safe in my hands."
> **ISAIAH 41:10**

Take a deep breath and read those words again . . . slowly.

They're from the book of Isaiah, in the Old Testament. Isaiah was giving the people a message from God . . . and it's a message that's true for us, too.

The truth is, all of us get scared from time to time. The things that scare you might not be the same things that scare your little brother or sister, your dad, or your best friend . . . but you've got some just the same.

Some people are scared of spiders. (Then again, some people keep them as pets!)
Some people are afraid of the dark.
Maybe for you it's thunderstorms, mean dogs, or creepy clowns.

Sometimes it isn't about "things." You might be afraid of losing a friendship, or of somebody you love dying. You might be afraid of trying something new—like a new sport or activity, or going to a new school.

Whew! There's a lot you can be nervous about. And fear is a completely natural feeling.

But you don't have to live in fear. You can **live fully alive**. When you feel scared, nervous, or afraid, you can replace that feeling with what God says is true:

"I am with you. . . .
I am your God.
I will make you strong and help you.
I will hold you safe in my hands."

You can face your fears and live courageously because God is with you!

Find a dry erase marker, or paper and pen. Write the four sentences from Isaiah 41:10 on the mirror you look at each morning and night when you brush your teeth. (Or you can write them on the piece of paper and then tape it to the mirror.) Practice reciting these truths to yourself first thing in the morning and right before bed.

DAY 23

**Do what's right because God
is always with you.**
Proverbs 28:1b

Just about every athlete has a pre-game routine. It's whatever gets them hyped up for the competition. Sometimes you see them wearing headphones, listening to their favorite song. Of course they're stretching out their muscles and warming up, but they're also getting their minds set on what's ahead.

What are some of *your* favorite songs? What would *you* listen to just before you hit the track, or the slopes, or the half pipe?

_____

_____

_____

We all need motivation sometimes. The right song can do that for you. In an even bigger way, your relationship with God can "fuel" you as you get ready for your day.

After all, doing what's right might *sound* simple, but . . .

If your parents tell you to stop playing your game and clean up your room, are you going to do it without complaining?

If you hear somebody saying something mean about a girl in your class, will you have the courage to defend her?

If your friends are looking at a video that you know is inappropriate, will you have the courage to say you're not going to watch it?

That takes a lot of strength, courage, and confidence. The good news is, God has all that and more—in abundance! You've got to remember that God is with you, and that He'll give you the strength you need to do what's right.

In **PROVERBS 28:1**, it says:

> *Those who do what is right are as bold as lions.*

Bold as lions! That means you're brave. You have no hesitation. You know what God wants you to do . . . and you do it. Even when it's hard.

The more you get in the habit of doing the right thing, the more confident you'll be. That's why it's so important to keep a close relationship with God—talking to Him and hearing from Him every single day.

Take a minute to decide on your "pre-game routine." What can you do each day before you head out the door to face the world?

Let God fill your heart each day with His strength and courage so you can do what's right!

DAY 24

Stay strong because God is always with you.
Isaiah 40:31

"Bring it on."
"I can do this."
"Stay strong."
"I know it'll be worth it."

Ask any elite athlete, and they'll tell you—they had a long road to get where they wanted to be. They had to set goals. They had to work hard. They had to fail along the way, then get back up and try again.

God has a BIG plan for your life.

And while you may know and believe that His way will be worth it in the long run, your whole life story is made up of a lot of different days—some good, and some bad. Some days you feel like you can do anything because of His power living inside you. Some days, nothing goes right . . . and you feel like giving up.

How are you feeling about God's plan today? On a scale of 1 to 10, are you feeling fired-up, full-throttle, "bring it on" level 10? Or are you down at 1? Somewhere in between?

1   2   3   4   5   6   7   8   9   10

The prophet Isaiah had something to say about that:

> *Those who trust in the LORD will receive new strength.*
> *They will fly as high as eagles. They will run and not*
> *get tired. They will walk and not grow weak.*
> **ISAIAH 40:31**

Talk about living fully alive! When you trust in the Lord, you will fly high, never grow tired, never get weak.

The hard part is . . .
Making choices that show you trust God every day.
Making the same **wise choices** whether you're feeling like a 3 or a 9.

Trusting that God holds your life story in His hands.
Leaving the outcome up to Him.

These verses hold some pretty awesome promises—especially for those times when you're exhausted. When it feels like you're the only one doing the right thing. When you make hard choices because the easy one was the wrong one. When you feel so much temptation you think you might burst.

God hasn't forgotten you. He sees what you're going through. He knows when things get tough. He understands the pressure you feel.

Ask Him for His **new strength** as you trust, push forward, and drop in!

DAY 25

See it through because God is always with you.
Nehemiah 6:3

If anyone knew about "seeing it through," it was a guy named Nehemiah. What he did was every bit as gnarly as a double black diamond run through the moguls . . . backwards!

(Gnarlier, actually.)

Nehemiah had a mission in life, and *nothing* was going to get in his way. He was going to finish what he started.

The back story? Nehemiah was living in Persia, working for the king, when he heard that the walls of his hometown, Jerusalem, were broken down. That meant God's people weren't safe, because back then, city walls protected the cities from invaders. Not only that, it was embarrassing for God's city to be in ruins.

So Nehemiah asked the king for permission to go to Jerusalem, and he got it! Once there, he got the people to help, and together, they started to rebuild the walls of the city.

Nehemiah pressed on, even though enemies tried to stop him. They didn't want the city to have strong walls. They asked Nehemiah to stop working, come down and talk to them. He said:

> *"I'm working on a huge project. So I can't get away. Why should the work stop while I leave it? Why should I go down and talk with you?"*
> **NEHEMIAH 6:3**

Nehemiah knew how important his work was. He knew that it was what God wanted him to do. He knew that God wanted him to lead the people for a reason.

We still talk about Nehemiah today because of the way he trusted God—even in the face of threats and challenges. He didn't stop when things got hard. He knew what he had to do, and he was courageous enough to see it through.

How about you? Is it sometimes hard for you to finish what you've started? All of us struggle with that at times . . . for so many reasons. You might get tired or frustrated. You might think, "Can't someone *else* do it?"

Remember, it's not just on your shoulders. God will give you the strength and confidence you need—just like He did for Nehemiah.

AMP IT UP

For this week's challenge, *you* get to be an interviewer. An extreme sports interviewer, that is!

Put on your beanie and your flannel if you have it . . . and come up with a funny reporter name. Like Star Edgerider. Or Thrash Breakstone.

Now find a "microphone" (which could be a spatula or a whisk from the kitchen). Put a sign on it with the Amped logo, like this.

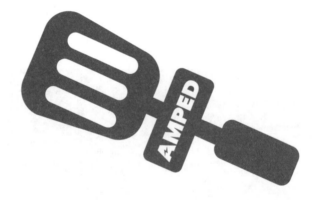

Don't forget a pen and a pad of paper . . . or you can use your device to video-record your interviewees (which would be pretty cool to have for later!).

So who are you interviewing? Great question. Someone who you trust, who follows God. Preferably someone older than you. It could be your parents . . . or maybe an older sibling, an aunt or uncle, or a grandparent. Maybe your coach or your Small Group Leader. Maybe the person who gave you this book!

Ask them these three questions. Be sure to write down or record their answers, because they're going to be super-valuable. You'll want to remember them.

1. Do you think following God means that you're living fully alive? Why?

///

///

///

2. Has there ever been a time when you needed to trust God in a difficult situation?

///

///

///

3. How did it help you to know that God was with you during that time?

///

///

///

SQUAD GOALS

6

WEEK 6

Squad Goals

From skydivers to synchronized swimmers, flag team to flag football, everybody needs a squad. We weren't meant to live fully . . . alone.

We need friends to cheer us on. We need friends to keep us focused. We need friends to help us make tough, but wise, choices. We need friends to help us trust Jesus. Friends are *there* for you, no matter what.

Not only that, you and your friends can reach for the same *squad goals*.
Together . . . you can help each other concentrate on the things that really matter.

Part of living fully alive is making sure you've got a squad you can count on.

So who's *your* squad?
Who encourages you to trust Jesus every day?

DAY 26

Find friends who help you trust Jesus.
John 1:45

When something good happens, you don't want to keep it to yourself. You've got to tell somebody!

If you watch an awesome movie, you can't wait to talk about it at school. (Spoiler alert!)
If you go to a new ice cream place that has the best flavors EVER, you've got to spread the word to all your friends.
If you see a snowboarder catch some sick air and land a frontside 360, you scream . . .

"Did you just see that?"

In John chapter 1, the Bible tells us about a guy named Philip who experienced something pretty amazing that he wanted to share with *his* friends.

> *Jesus was just getting started choosing His disciples—the friends who would travel with Him, serve with Him, and share the good news about Him. Jesus saw Philip, and He simply said, "Follow me."*
> **JOHN 1:43**

That was enough for Philip. Of course he said, "Yes!" He knew there was something special about Jesus—that Jesus was the Savior they had been waiting for. But Philip didn't just keep all of this to himself. He said this to his friend Nathanael:

> *"We have found the one whom Moses wrote about in the Law. The prophets also wrote about him. He is Jesus of Nazareth, the son of Joseph."*
> **JOHN 1:45**

Philip wanted Nathanael to know about Jesus, too. Jesus really was the Promised One, and He was about to change their lives *forever!*

Just like Philip, you can encourage your friends to trust Jesus. And your friends can do that for you, too.

When you find friends who help you trust Jesus, you're surrounding yourself with a rock-solid squad. You're spending time with others who've chosen to build their lives on what's most important—their relationship with Jesus.

You can pray for each other.
You can encourage each other.
You can remind each other to make wise choices and live out what you believe.

You can live each day with confidence, knowing you've got a squad to support you!

Are there people in your squad now who help you trust Jesus? How about people who maybe *should* be in your squad because you know they have a solid relationship with Jesus? List some of those friends here:

DAY 27

Choose the right friends.
Proverbs 12:26a

Really quick: Draw a picture of how you met one of your friends.

Did you know that you get to *choose* your friends?

Maybe it doesn't always seem like that's the case. You probably hang out at school with whoever's in your class. At home or on the weekends, you probably spend most of your time with friends who live in your neighborhood or apartment complex. Maybe you hang out with some friends just because your parents are friends with *their* parents.

If you think about it, though, you do spend more time with some friends than others. It could be because you think they're cool or fun, or maybe you have a lot in common with them. You spend so much time with them that they become your crew . . . your squad . . . your BFFs.

Look what the Bible says about friendships in **PROVERBS 12:26**:

> *Godly people are careful about the friends they choose*

If you want to live fully alive and follow Jesus, choose friends who . . .

- want to follow Jesus, too.
- think what's most important to you is what's most important to them.
- will be a good influence on you (and you'll be a good influence on them).

Of course, you can have all kinds of different friends. That's important, too. Just because you have a closer friendship with some people, that doesn't mean you can't still be friendly and kind to everyone else. You can learn a lot from everyone you meet. But when you're choosing who to spend most of your time with—who you'll really look up to—you've got to choose carefully.

Talk to your parents about this. Ask them for advice. See which friends of yours they'd like you to spend more (or less) time with—and why. After all, they probably know you better than you'd like to admit. They can see what kind of impact your friends are having on you even more clearly than you can. They can even help you make a plan for how to spend more or less time with a person while still being friendly about it—like how to handle situations in the lunch room or recess.

Your friendships will affect your life more than you might realize. So do everything you can to choose them carefully!

DAY 28

Choose friends who are wise.
Proverbs 13:20

What could be better than winning a gold medal?

What could be better than winning the lottery?

What could be better than doing whatever you wanted, whenever you wanted, and having all the money in the world?

Wisdom.

Don't believe me? Check out **PROVERBS 16:16**:

> *It is much better to get wisdom than gold. It is much better to choose understanding than silver.*

Wisdom is also a REALLY great thing to look for in a friend. So does that mean you should be on the lookout for friends who are really smart? Not exactly. Wisdom is different from intelligence. Intelligence is knowing facts. Wisdom is finding out what you should do and doing it. Wise people look for what God wants them to do, and then they make it happen.

Solomon knew how important wisdom is in friendships. In **PROVERBS 13:20**, he wrote,

> *Walk with wise people and become wise. A companion of foolish people suffers harm.*

"Walk with" means "spend time with." Over time, you'll probably start to think and act like the people you walk with . . . and that could be a really good thing, or a really bad thing. If you hang out with wise people, they'll make you wise. But if you spend time with UNwise people, you'll start making unwise choices yourself.

So how do you find wise people?
- Look at the way they **act**. Do they make decisions without thinking? Or do they stop and think about how their actions will affect other people?
- Look at the way they **talk**. If you used the kind of words they do, would you be proud of yourself? Or embarrassed?
- Look at the way they **listen**. Do they act like they know it all? Or do they ask questions instead?

Take a minute to think about your circle of friends. Who's a wise friend that you could get to know better? Is there anyone who maybe shouldn't be getting as much of your time and attention?

Remember—if you surround yourself with wise friends, then you're set up to WIN (a different kind of lottery)!

DAY 29

Choose friends who have your back.
Ecclesiastes 4:9-10

Have you ever gone up a climbing wall? It can be pretty intimidating to go straight up like that.

One thing's for sure, though. You feel so much more confident after testing your weight on the safety harness—when you know you can't possibly fall. Even if you never slip, it's nice to have that harness there to help you feel safe and secure.

Good friends are like that, too. God knew we would need other people who encourage us and cheer us on in life—who support us when we feel weak. He knew that all of us would need people we can be real and honest with—who we can lean on completely. People who can handle the weight of all our different sides: the good, the bad, and the ugly.

Good friends are there for us in the tough times—like when we mess up, or when we're feeling down. They forgive us. They give us hope. They catch us like a harness so there's no chance we can fall.

Check out these verses from the book of Ecclesiastes:

> *Two people are better than one. They can help each other in everything they do. Suppose either of them falls down. Then the one can help the other one up.*
> **ECCLESIASTES 4:9-10**

That's a great image of friendship: one friend helping another friend up. But the verse isn't just talking about tripping over a tree root or slipping on ice.

The verse is also talking about when your life seems to fall down. When you're facing a tough choice or made a bad choice, when you feel lonely and unlikeable, when things seem out of your control.

That's when you know whether you've chosen friends who have your back, or "fair-weather friends"—friends who are only there in the good times, when you don't need support at all.

As you think more about and become more intentional about who you spend the most time with, try to imagine how your friends would support you during the hard times. (Or maybe you don't have to imagine, because they've already been through some tough stuff with you.)

And remember, it's not all about you! You can be that kind of friend for someone else, too. You can be the one reaching down to help a friend off the ground. That could be one of the biggest ways that God uses you—to show love and support to someone who really needs it.

DAY 30

Choose friends who make you better.
Proverbs 27:17

Have you ever wondered how a skate blade gets so sharp? After all, it needs to be able to slice through the ice without getting caught or stuck.

(With the help of an adult, look up some Ice Cross videos and you'll see why the blade is so important. Seriously, they're fun!)

If you take your skates to a shop, they have professional sharpening machines to make sure your blades are ready for the rink . . . or the slope.

But did you know your squad can "sharpen" you, too?

> *As iron sharpens iron, so one person sharpens another.*
> **PROVERBS 27:17**

In other words, we make each other *better*. A dull ice blade is going to be catastrophic, but the same blade with a little sharpening will work miracles. In the same way, each of us needs some help focusing on the things that matter most.

Think about your very best friends. Why are they so important to you? Is it because you've been through so much together? Is it because they always listen to you when you have a problem? Do they always laugh at your jokes? Do they make you feel good about life in general? It's probably all of those things.

Another reason friends are so important is that we admire them. We look up to them. We want to *be* like them. We might even follow their lead and do something good because we've been able to see them in action. That's what the verse means by "sharpening" each other.

It also means that we might challenge our friends, or they might challenge us. If we find ourselves making an unwise choice, they can remind us of what's true. They can put us back on track . . . and we can do the same for them. We're not afraid to listen because we trust what they have to say. We know they're "sharpening" us because they care.

Take a few minutes to think about your friendships and pray. Ask God to help you create great friendships—where you and your friends can "sharpen" each other as you grow.

AMP IT UP

Now's the perfect chance to thank your squad!

Usually we only write thank-you notes when we get a gift. But what if you did that for your friends right now, just to encourage them?

Let's put it this way. How do you think it would make *you* feel to get something like this?

To: //

I'm glad you're my friend.
I think you're hilarious.
Thanks for praying for me when I was sick.
Thanks for always having my back.
You always help me follow God.
You're awesome!

Here's what you do. Carefully cut out the postcards on the next couple of pages, and choose four friends to give them to. On the back of each card, write down four or five things that you appreciate about each friend. Be sure to tell them how they encourage you in your relationship with God.

Don't miss this chance to thank your friends for helping you *live fully alive!*

AMPED
THANKS FOR BEING IN MY SQUAD

AMPED
THANKS FOR BEING IN MY SQUAD

PLACE
STAMP
HERE

PLACE
STAMP
HERE

AMPED

THANKS FOR BEING IN MY SQUAD

AMPED

THANKS FOR BEING IN MY SQUAD

PLACE
STAMP
HERE

PLACE
STAMP
HERE

IN THE ZONE

7

WEEK 7

In the Zone

You need total concentration to do any kind of extreme sport. You can't get distracted by your nerves or the fact that you didn't eat enough for breakfast.
You can't let your mind stray for one millisecond.

You need to be hyper-focused—**in the zone.**

Picture it. You're sliding full-speed down an alpine coaster . . . kite surfing in shark-infested waters . . . or mountain biking a summit ridge with a 1,000-foot drop on either side. You've got to *focus*, because you don't have any room for error.

You've got to stay focused in life, too. You need to live on purpose each day. If your goal is to live an AMPED life by following Jesus, you can't let yourself get distracted and take your eyes off Him.

What distracts *you* from focusing on Jesus?

This week, we'll look at the life of one of Jesus' friends named Peter. We'll discover a few key moments when Peter learned how important it is to stay in the zone and keep your focus on Jesus.

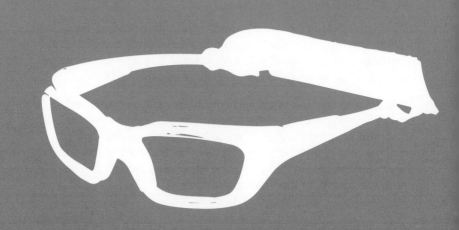

DAY 31

Stay focused on Jesus.
Matthew 14:29-31

There's this Olympic sport called the biathlon. And just like a *triathlon* combines three activities (swimming, biking, and running), the *biathlon* combines two activities: cross-country skiing and target shooting.

You're probably thinking, "Wait . . . *what?*"
"What does skiing have to do with shooting?"
"How can you ski with a gun on your back?"
"How can you shoot with skis on?"
"But, *why?*"

The biathlon seems like a very strange combination of activities to excel in. Until you think of the moment the athlete looks through the scope and tries to shoot a very small black circle 160 feet away.

Talk about having to be in the zone! This athlete is standing on slippery ice, in skis (*made* to slip on the ice), totally out of breath from skiing on flat, sometimes *uphill* terrain (I had no idea it was possible to ski uphill because . . . well, physics).

They have to stay balanced and completely still, control their breath, and focus only on the target. Not the course they just skied, not whether they're in first or last place, not wondering what the rest of the course will be like. For that part of the race, they can think of one thing and one thing only. And it requires complete control of their mind *and* body.

One of Jesus' disciples, Peter, learned a thing or two about staying focused in his time following Jesus. He probably wasn't good on skis and biathlon guns (or any guns for that matter, because guns hadn't been invented). But he practiced being *in the zone* in a pretty radical way.

It all happened after Jesus miraculously fed a crowd of over 5,000 people with just one boy's dinner. Everyone was pretty amped up after seeing this miracle, and Jesus' 12 closest disciples were eager to get with Jesus and recount the incredible day they'd had.

But Jesus needed a moment to connect with God, alone. So He sent His friends out in a boat while He went up on a mountainside to pray. Hours passed. Soon the disciples were out in the middle of the lake, in the middle of the night, with the wind howling and the waves pounding the boat—wondering how Jesus would get to them.

Suddenly, they saw Someone *walking on the water* toward them. *"It's a ghost!"* they cried out **MATTHEW 14:26**. But it was Jesus! He called out to them, *"Be brave! It is I. Don't be afraid"* **MATTHEW 14:27**.

Peter wanted to be sure. He said, *"Lord, is it you? . . . If it is, tell me to come to you on the water"* **MATTHEW 14:28**.

Jesus told Peter to come, and so Peter got out of the boat and started *walking on the water toward Jesus*. Imagine what that must have been like! In the darkness, in the middle of the lake, with the waves crashing around him . . . Peter set his eyes on Jesus and walked on the water toward his Savior.

But it didn't last. Peter took his eyes off Jesus and looked at the wind instead. He started to get scared. He started to sink! But right away, Jesus caught him. *"Your faith is so small!"* [Jesus] said. *"Why did you doubt me?"* **MATTHEW 14:31**.

It's easy to look at the "wind and the waves" around us—homework, tournaments, challenges with our friends and family, etc. It's easy to get scared or doubt there's ever a way out, instead of focusing on Jesus. But when we **stay focused on Jesus**, those pieces of life don't seem quite as scary. And it's easier to trust that our Savior has it all under control.

Take a minute to pray and ask God to help you stay focused on Him.

DAY 32

Jesus wants you to follow Him.
Matthew 4:18-20

If you want to get really good at any sport, you have to listen to your coaches and trainers. They know how to get you to do your very best.
They can see things you can't see.
They know things you don't know.
They will lead you where you need to go.

And where you want to go is . . .

the playoffs!
the finals!
the championship!

So you'll do whatever your coaches say is necessary to meet that goal.

That's what it was like for Peter when he first met Jesus:

> One day Jesus was walking beside the Sea of Galilee. There he saw two brothers, Simon Peter and his brother Andrew. They were throwing a net into the lake, because they were fishermen. "Come and follow me," Jesus said. "I will send you out to fish for people." At once they left their nets and followed him.
> **MATTHEW 4:18-20**

Circle the words "at once." There was no hesitation! Peter and Andrew left what they were doing to follow Jesus. They could see that He was the One to help them get where they wanted to be: free, accepted, loved, part of something BIG. They trusted Jesus and they never looked back.

How about you? Are you hesitating in any way in your relationship with Jesus? Are you hitting the pause button? Is there something you feel like He wants you to do, but you just don't want to do it?

If we're honest, all of us feel stuck sometimes. We get distracted. We get fearful. We don't know if we can really live out what we believe.

- Maybe you're in an argument with your sister, and you don't *want* to forgive her.
- Maybe you're having a hard time staying focused in class. You find yourself talking with your friends instead of respecting your teacher.
- Maybe you don't feel like praying because you're sad or disappointed about something that didn't go your way.

Even in those situations, you can choose to trust and follow Jesus. **Jesus wants you to follow Him because He knows what's best for you.** He loves you! And He's giving you the same clear, simple message that He gave Peter and Andrew: *"Come and follow me."* **MATTHEW 4:19**

DAY 33

Focus on who Jesus really is.
Matthew 16:15-18

Do you go to church each Sunday? Some Sundays? Rarely ever?

What do you love most about it? The music? The people? The stories?

Sometimes, the more often we go to church, the more likely we are to associate Jesus with:
Dressing up
Standing up and sitting down
Listening
Praying out loud
Donuts and Goldfish

The more we go to church, the easier it is to think Jesus only exists in the church building. And our lives the rest of the week have very little—maybe nothing—to do with Him.

Now, that's *not* a knock on going to church. It's just a reminder to keep focused on the most important *part* of church. It's totally okay to indulge in a donut hole (or 10). It's normal to peek while praying every now and then. It's perfectly acceptable to play tag in the hallways. (Okay, maybe not that last one.)

The most important part is the knowledge and attitude you carry with you when you leave your church building: Jesus is the Son of God. He loves you. He wants you to follow Him. You can trust Him no matter what. When you stay **focused on who Jesus really is**, it changes everything about your life—and I'm not just talking about Sundays.

Let's fast-forward in Peter's story, to a conversation he and the other disciples had with Jesus. (This was after the whole walking-on-water part.)

"Who do you say I am?" [Jesus asked.]

> *Simon Peter answered, "You are the Messiah.*
> *You are the Son of the living God."*
> **MATTHEW 16:15-16**

Ding! Ding! Ding! Peter had answered Jesus correctly.
He was *absolutely sure* that Jesus really is who He said He is:
the Son of God.

After all, Peter and the other disciples had a front-row seat to all that Jesus had done. They had seen Him perform miracles and heal people (including Peter's own mother-in-law!). It was easy to see that He was the One.

Following Jesus is a way of life. Your relationship with Him is 24/7. It's easy to get distracted by all kinds of things. But when you **focus on who Jesus really is**—the Messiah, the Son of the living God, your Savior—that changes the way you live each day.

You don't just do the right thing because you have to, or because you're supposed to. You do the right thing because you love Jesus and want to be like Him.

You serve others—like the Son of the living God did.
You show kindness to people who are overlooked—like your Savior did.
You even choose to love your enemies—like Jesus did.

Focus on who Jesus really is. Let Him guide you each day to become more and more like Him.

DAY 34

Focus on what you know is true.
Luke 22:59-62

Jesus made insane amounts of fish appear in nets.
Jesus healed a man with leprosy.
Jesus raised a man from the dead.
Jesus stopped a raging storm.
Jesus made a blind man see for the first time.
Jesus fed more than 5,000 people with one small picnic dinner.
Jesus walked on water.
Jesus helped *Peter* to walk on water.

After everything Peter had seen and experienced, you'd think his faith in Jesus would have been rock-solid—that nothing could ever shake it. That's what *he* thought, too. But there was no way he could have prepared for what was about to happen.

One day, Jesus gathered His friends together for a meal. He told them He was about to be arrested . . . that He was leaving them. Instead of ruling as king, like they'd all expected Him to do, He was about to suffer and die—like a criminal.

It didn't make sense. But Peter tried to be brave. *"Lord, I am ready to go with you to prison and to death,"* he said **LUKE 22:33**. But things were about to get . . .

blurry.

Jesus saw how eager Peter was to back Him up, but He had some bad news for His friend.

> *Jesus answered, "I tell you, Peter, you will say three times that you don't know me. And you will do it before the rooster crows today."*
> **LUKE 22:34**

It sounded ridiculous. Peter had said he was willing to *die* for Jesus. How could he deny even *knowing* Jesus—*three times?*

Then the unthinkable actually happened. Jesus *was* arrested, and Peter followed from a distance. He had just sat down with some people in a courtyard when a servant girl glared closely at Peter and said, *"This man was with Jesus"* **LUKE 22:56**. Peter was scared and confused. He denied it: *"I don't know him"* **LUKE 22:57**.

Later on, someone else saw Peter and said, *"You also are one of them"* **LUKE 22:58**. Suddenly, it seemed like everyone was out to get him. Again, Peter denied it.

Later, another person spoke up: *"This fellow must have been with Jesus"* **LUKE 22:59**. Peter could sense that he was in danger. *"I don't know what you're talking about!"* he cried **LUKE 22:60**. Just then, a rooster crowed and Jesus looked directly at Peter. Peter remembered what Jesus had said—that Peter would deny Him three times—and he broke down and cried. Jesus had been right.

Peter certainly *thought* he could stay strong for Jesus. He knew what was true: that Jesus was the all-powerful Son of God. But when Jesus was arrested, everything Peter knew seemed to crumble before his eyes. He got scared. He couldn't see clearly anymore.

Life gets blurry sometimes. Things happen that make you feel scared and alone. When they do, that's when it's most important to **focus on what you know is true**. Focus on the fact that Jesus loves you. He hasn't forgotten you. You might not be able to see a way out. But you can **trust** that the Son of God is right there with you.

DAY 35

Jesus can help you refocus your life.
John 21:17

Ask any inline skater or ice climber or longboarder. Bumps and bruises are just part of the deal. Even with protective gear, you'll end up with some cuts and scrapes.

So what do you do when you crash and burn? You might sit there in a daze for a minute. You might shed a tear or two (because it *hurts!*). But you've got to get back up again. You've got to get bandaged up, rest up, and then get back out there for more.

The truth is, all of us fall—or get knocked down—sometimes. We mess up. We forget to trust God when we're scared or angry. We might even feel far from Him because we're ashamed of what we've done wrong.

Think about how Peter must have felt. He *thought* he could stand with Jesus until the end . . . but when things got tough, he denied that he even knew Him.

Of course, we know what happened next. Jesus died on the cross to pay the price for the sins of the world. But He didn't stay dead. On the third day, His friends discovered that the tomb was *empty*. Jesus had come back to life! He proved that He really is God's Son, and that everything that had happened—His arrest, His beating, His humiliation, His crucifixion, His *resurrection*—was part of God's great rescue plan.

Jesus appeared to His friends a couple of times after that, including one time when He had breakfast with them on the beach. (Check it out in John 21.) During breakfast that morning, Jesus took time to speak to Peter. He asked him three times: *"Do you love me?"* **JOHN 21:15, 16, 17**. Each time, Peter said, *"You know that I love you"* **JOHN 21:15, 16, 17**. It was like Jesus was asking Peter one time for each of the three times Peter had denied Him. Jesus was telling Peter that He forgave him for each denial—because He knew what was really in Peter's heart. He knew Peter loved Him, even if Peter had messed up.

But part of Jesus' response to Peter's statements might sound a little odd to us. "Feed my sheep," Jesus basically said three times. But He wasn't really talking about *sheep* sheep. He was talking about *us*. (Remember that whole God-and-Jesus-as-a-shepherd business?)

Jesus meant that He wanted Peter to lead His *people*—the church. Peter might have denied Jesus three times. But instead of pushing Peter to the side—instead of punishing him and never letting him recover from his mistakes—Jesus forgave Peter and trusted him with a really important job. Jesus refocused Peter's life and reminded him of all that He had chosen him to do.

If you mess up, don't hide from God. He's your safe place. Talk to Him and tell Him about it. You know for SURE that He'll forgive you. We all mess up. It's not all over after one (or 20) mistakes, no matter how big. **Jesus can help you refocus your life.**

AMP IT UP

Peter's life was full of ups and downs. Yours probably is, too. It takes a lot of hard work to stay *in the zone* and keep your focus on Jesus. That's why faith is a journey!

Have you heard of the Appalachian Trail? It's a hiking trail through the Appalachian Mountains. But it's not just any hiking trail. It's LONG. Like around 2,200 miles long. Like Georgia to Maine long. Hikers on the Appalachian Trail really have to stay in the zone if they want to reach their goal of hiking the whole trail. Luckily, there are white blazes painted on trees that they can follow.

The trail stretches all the way from Springer Mountain, Georgia, to Mount Katahdin, Maine. On the way, it passes through 14 states. (In some places, you're hiking with one foot in Tennessee and the other one in North Carolina!)

Kids as young as five years old have hiked the entire AT. And it's *not* an easy journey. Hikers sleep in tents or shelters. They go to the bathroom in the woods. They get to experience things people in the towns can only dream of—glorious sunny days on grassy mountaintops with views in every direction. But they also have to trudge through ice, snow, rain, and mud. They have to carry everything they need in a backpack that's almost as big as they are. They're always on the lookout for tree roots, loose rocks, or snakes underfoot.

It's all worth it to reach the sign at the end, on top of Mount Katahdin.

One fun tradition among "through-hikers" is to go by a trail name instead of your real name. Usually it's a name other hikers choose for you. Here are some examples:

- Sasquatch
- Salamander
- Bambi Magnet
- Tye-Dye
- Banana Split

Fun fact: Peter sort of had a trail name himself. His name means "The Rock."

Think for a minute—what would you want *your* trail name to be? Write it here, just for fun.

NEVER FLYING SOLO

8

WEEK 8

Never Flying Solo

It's hard to say what the most extreme sport would be. But wingsuit flying has got to be up there.

Basically, you wear a special kind of suit that makes your body shape flatter so you don't just fall through the air. You have more lift. Then, you use a parachute to make sure you have a safe, gentle landing.

Of course, wingsuit flying is extremely dangerous. Typical speeds are around 120 miles per hour, which is twice as fast as a car zooming down the freeway! Plus, there are a million little things that have to go just right for you to have a successful jump. (Note: successful = alive.)

A regular day in your life probably doesn't seem as exciting (or terrifying) as a wingsuit jump. But still, there's so much more at stake each day than you might realize. Every choice you make, every interaction you have with other people—it matters.

The best part is knowing that you're **never flying solo**. Sometimes you might *feel* alone. You might feel like you're the only one doing the right thing. You might have to face some pretty big challenges. But you never have to face them alone. Jesus is always with you—holding you up—lifting you higher.

How can you face challenges knowing Jesus is with you? Let's talk about that this week.

DAY 36

When Jesus is with you, you can face anything.
Acts 4:18-20

Fill in each blank letter in these dynamic duos to discover the most unstoppable team there ever was!

Mashed potatoes and Grav____

Shoes and S____cks

Sweet and So____r

Hide ____ ____ ____ Seek

Peanut Butter and ____elly

Pencil and Pap____r

Hugs and Kis____es

Ketchup and M____stard

Macaroni and Chee____e

Answer: ____ ____ ____   ____ ____ ____   ____ ____ ____ ____ ____

Remember Peter? The guy we talked about all last week? Well, I've got one more Peter story for you. One that happened after all the others. At this point, Jesus had gone up to Heaven. He had sent His Spirit to the disciples—to live inside them and to guide them.

Peter began to speak boldly and confidently about Jesus. He taught the people how they could turn away from their sins and believe in Jesus . . . and *thousands* of them did.

One day, Peter and John were approaching the temple gate, and they saw a man begging for money. The man couldn't walk. Peter told him he didn't have any silver or gold, but he said to the man, *"Get up and walk"* **Acts 3:6**. And the man did!

A crowd started to gather. Peter told them that he didn't heal the man with his own power; God had healed him. Peter also shared the whole story of Jesus, which made the religious leaders furious! (They didn't believe that Jesus is really the Son of God.) They had Peter and John thrown in jail.

The leaders sent for Peter and John to question them, and Peter told them that they had healed the man in the name of Jesus.

Now, look at what the leaders noticed about Peter and John:

> *The leaders saw how bold Peter and John were. They also realized that Peter and John were ordinary men with no training. This surprised the leaders. They realized that **these men had been with Jesus***
> **ACTS 4:13** (emphasis added)

They called Peter and John in again, and they ordered them not to speak about Jesus anymore. But Peter said, *"We have to speak about the things we've seen and heard"* **Acts 4:20**.

Wow—this was the same Peter who had once denied that he even *knew* Jesus! What had changed? What do you think made him so bold, even in the face of such powerful leaders who were commanding him to keep quiet?

Peter was confident because **Jesus was with him**. The leaders could see that for themselves. He was filled with God's Holy Spirit (verse 8). He wasn't flying solo. He knew that **when Jesus is with you, you can face anything**!

You can be confident like Peter and John. You've seen God do some amazing things in your life, and you've seen how He carried you through the tough times, too. You know that He'll be there to help you face *anything* that might come your way!

YOU AND JESUS = UNSTOPPABLE

DAY 37

You can face anything with contentment.
Philippians 4:11-13

In the space below, draw some of your favorite things. It could be video games, or toys, or even your favorite foods.

My Faves

Isn't it funny that we could play video games for hours, but it's never enough? When your mom calls you for dinner, you never want to push pause.

Maybe you collect toys, or action figures, or Beanie Boos. When your birthday comes around, you know exactly what you want: just one more!

It doesn't matter how big the pizza is—you always feel like you could eat one more slice.

Life is like that, too. We always seem to want *more*. We also want things to be *easy*. But part of living fully alive is living with **contentment**.

Contentment is an attitude shift.
It's not about getting enough stuff so you can finally be happy.
It's deciding that you have enough.
It's not about wishing you had more of something. It's deciding that God has a reason for what you already have.
It's not about wishing your life could be easier. It's deciding that God has a purpose for what your life is like right now.

Look at what Paul wrote in his letter to the Philippians. He said that he had found the *secret* of contentment.

> *I have learned to be content no matter what happens to me. I know what it's like not to have what I need. I also know what it's like to have more than I need. I have learned the secret of being content no matter what happens. I am content whether I am well fed or hungry. I am content whether I have more than enough or not enough. I can do all this by the power of Christ. He gives me strength.*
> **PHILIPPIANS 4:11-13**

So what was Paul's secret? Jesus!

Jesus is with you, too. And because He's always with you, **you can face anything with contentment.** You can face *anything*— and be truly joyful—because He gives you His power and strength.

This week, whenever you start to *really* want something, practice saying this truth to yourself:

"I have enough."

If that's hard to believe at first, ask God to help you think of all that you already have instead of focusing on what you think is missing.

Talk about upside down. James knew it was a pretty wild expectation, so he went on to explain himself.

Your faith will be tested. You know that when this happens it will produce in you the strength to continue. And you must allow this strength to finish its work. Then you will be all you should be. You will have everything you need.
JAMES 1:3-4

So, what James is saying is—when you break your leg or get the flu or find yourself in big trouble, your life will still go on. You'll find a way to keep on living, even though up until that point you swore you'd die without soccer or if you had to miss that sleepover. But you're stronger than you think. Jesus is right there with you to help you. And when you have to be strong, you'll find that you really do have all you need in Him.

Following Jesus doesn't mean your life is going to be easy. But with Jesus, we're never facing our challenges alone. In fact, our challenges actually help us to trust and rely on Him more, because we wouldn't have the strength to face them ourselves. We need HIS strength to overcome them. And that gives us a deep, satisfying sense of joy that we couldn't experience any other way.

Facing challenges with joy—it's possible! Even if it seems a little upside down.

DAY 38

You can face anything with joy.
James 1:2-4

Hey there!

Don't worry, there's nothing wrong with your book. It's supposed to be like this.

So why is this page upside down? Well, in a way, that's kind of what it's like to follow Jesus. He's constantly changing the way we think about things and turning them upside down . . . in a good way!

Jesus tells us to . . .

put others ahead of ourselves.

be content when we don't think we have everything we need.

love our enemies.

Here's another "upside down" kind of thought. It comes from a letter written by James (Jesus' half-brother).

My brothers and sisters, you will face all kinds of trouble. When you do, think of it as pure joy.
JAMES 1:2

Huh? We're supposed to think of our troubles as pure joy?

"Hooray! I broke my leg and can't play my favorite sport for the rest of the season!"

"Yippee! I've always wanted the flu!"

"Hallelujah! I'm grounded for a month and I'm so happy I could scream!"

DAY 39

You can face anything because Jesus gives you peace.
John 14:27

Have you ever watched a race—maybe at the Olympics— where an athlete came up just a little bit short? Maybe it was a swimming competition where one of swimmers came in fourth place and missed winning a medal by a fingernail.

It's always hard to lose. But Olympic athletes train years and years for that *one* shot to compete. Their loss is even more crushing.

You know what that swimmer does next, though? They don't give up. They know that the next Olympics are four years away. They get to work, practicing and training for the next one. They know what they have to do to be able to compete again for their country.

So how do you do it? How do you keep your chin up and keep fighting when life gets you down?

It's all about your goal. *What are you fighting for?*

You see, athletes have a goal that keeps them motivated. It's the thrill and the challenge of competition. Your goal is even *more* important—you're trying to make the most out of the life God has given you.

It would be tough to do that if you were by yourself. You'd get knocked around and discouraged. Small problems would seem like big problems, and big problems would seem almost too big to handle. Thankfully, you're *not* alone. You know Jesus is with you. And He can give you something that's even more powerful than you might realize: His peace.

Here's what Jesus said to His friends, the disciples:

> *"I leave my peace with you. I give my peace to you. I do not give it to you as the world does. Do not let your hearts be troubled. And do not be afraid."*
> **JOHN 14:27**

The next time something knocks you down and makes you feel discouraged, take a minute to pray and thank God for His peace. Choose not to let your heart feel troubled or afraid. Instead, remind yourself that **you can face anything because Jesus gives you peace**.

DAY 40

Stay connected to Jesus so you can face anything.
John 15:5

Do you still have the "Stay Connected" tag on your charging cord? (We talked about that in the Week 1 "Amp It Up" challenge.)

Remember, you can stay connected to God by praying, reading your Bible, and talking to other people about Him. Hopefully that tag has been a good reminder for you to do that these past few weeks.

Jesus actually talked about this exact thing with the disciples—except He wasn't talking about a charging cord for a laptop or a phone. He was using an example that His friends would have easily understood: fruit growing on a vine.

Here's what Jesus said:

> *"I am the vine. You are the branches. If you remain joined to me, and I to you, you will bear a lot of fruit. You can't do anything without me."*
> **JOHN 15:5**

In other words, you can't cut a branch off a vine and expect that branch to still produce fruit. It won't produce anything. It'll just sit there! But if the branch is connected to the main vine, it can get the nutrients and everything it needs to grow the fruit.

You're not alone. You're connected to the Vine! And you'll grow all kinds of fruit if you stay connected to Jesus. Not grapes and kiwis and watermelons, but the fruit of the *Spirit*:

Love	**Joy**	**Peace**
Patience	**Kindness**	**Goodness**
Faithfulness	**Gentleness**	**Self-control**

I don't know about you, but those are the words I really hope people use to describe me. And the kinds of words I want to be able to use to describe my friends!

So how do you stay connected to Jesus, the Vine, again? By talking *to* Him, talking *about* Him, and spending time reading your Bible.

All of us need to grow, every single day. And when we grow stronger and stronger in our relationship with God, we're becoming more and more ready for whatever life throws our way.

It makes sense; we can only *live fully alive* if we're connected to the One who gives us life to begin with!

AMP IT UP

Let's take this outside again. Is there somewhere you can go that's quiet and relaxing? Maybe you could sit under a tree in your backyard, or maybe your mom or dad would be willing to take you to the park.

Before you go, see if you have any grapes in your house. Wash a few and put them in a zipper bag. (A juice box would work, too. Really you just need something fruity and yummy.)

See you outside!

Okay, have you found your spot? Go ahead and get your snack out, and we'll get started. The grapes are to remind you about what Jesus said. Remember, He's the Vine, and we need to stay joined to Him if we want to produce a lot of fruit (of the Spirit) and live to the fullest.

Take 5-10 minutes to really talk to God. Try not to be in a rush or think about anything except what you're saying to Him.

Eat those grapes while you pray, because they're delicious!
Tell Him what's going on in your heart.
Tell Him what you've been learning and thinking about as you go through this book.
Ask Him to help you face whatever hard things are going on in your life right now.
Thank Him for giving you His joy and peace.
It's great to take time to really pray, isn't it? You don't ever have to fly solo, because God is always there to talk.

AMPLIFIED

9

WEEK 9

Amplified

By now, you have a pretty good idea of what it looks like to live fully alive.

You know that an AMPED life is supercharged, because it's based on God's one and only Son.

You know that God can use you and your unique story—no matter how "goofy" it may seem.

You know that God's strength is the anchor for your life.

You know that with God, impossible is nothing.

You know that you can "drop in" and live courageously when you trust God.

You know that your squad can encourage you to follow God.

You know you've got to be *in the zone* when life tries to distract you.

You know that you're never flying solo, because Jesus is with you.

The most exciting part of all is that your life isn't just about you. You're living for something much bigger. You're part of God's Big Story: the story that started when God made everything out of nothing.

When you take all of what you've learned and you put it into practice, you can amplify what God is doing in your life. If you've been in a band or around music at all, you know what an amp is. It's a device you can plug into to make an instrument LOUDER. And just like an amp, the tools you learned in this book can help make your life louder, bigger, greater. They can help you live loud, for Jesus! They can help you show the people around you what a difference Jesus can make—in your life, and theirs.

So let's put it all together.

How would you live if you believed what God says is true?

DAY 41

Live like you believe what God says is true.
Romans 8:38-39

Who are you a fan of? It could be an athlete, a musician, an actor, or anyone. Who is it that you would say these words to: "I. Am. Your. BIGGEST. Fan!"

Write your answer here:

When you're someone's biggest fan, it doesn't matter what anyone else says or thinks. It doesn't matter how many points they score, how many championships they win, how many of your birthday parties they perform at . . . you are and will always be their *biggest* fan.

Did you know that you also have a *biggest* (literally) fan? GOD! You are SO important to God. He's your biggest Fan. No matter what. How does it feel to know that He's *that* crazy about you?

In his letter to the Romans, Paul explained just how much God loves us.

> *I am absolutely sure that not even death or life can separate us from God's love. Not even angels or demons, the present or the future, or any powers can separate us. Not even the highest places or the lowest, or anything else in all creation can separate us. Nothing at all can ever separate us from God's love. That's because of what Christ Jesus our Lord has done.*
> **ROMANS 8:38-39**

Nothing can separate you from God's love! When Jesus died on the cross, He made it possible for you to have a relationship with God that isn't based on what *you* do. It's about what Jesus did *for* you.

You don't ever have to worry if God will stop loving you. He won't. You don't ever have to worry if God will forgive you. He will. You don't ever have to worry about what might or might not happen in your life. God has a plan. Your biggest Fan is in control.

If you didn't believe that, how would you act? Afraid. Anxious. Unsure.
But when you DO believe it, you're brave . . . confident . . . and joyful.

Color in the parachute on the next couple of pages and write in the words, "Nothing can separate us." God will carry you through whatever you might face in life. *Nothing* can separate you from Him.

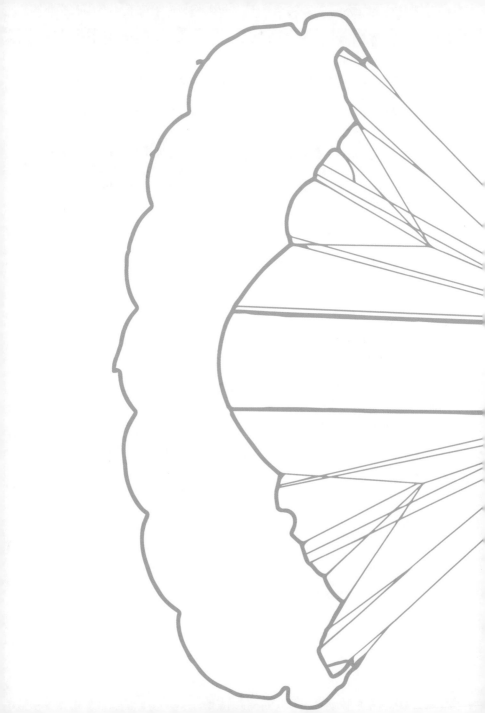

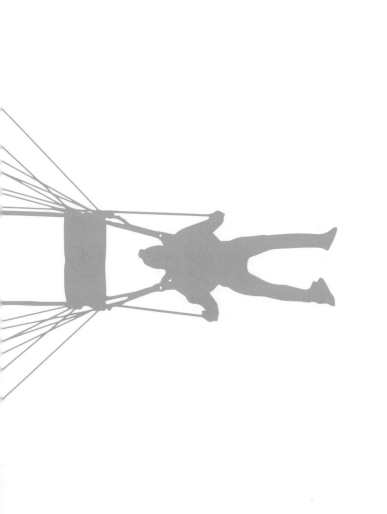

DAY 42

Your life can point others to God.
Psalm 115:1

How do you celebrate when you win something? What do you do when your favorite team wins a game?

Some people high-five their friends.
Some people pump their fist or point to the sky.
Some people yell at the top of their lungs.

It's exciting to be in a stadium and hear thousands of people break into applause. Maybe you've imagined what it would be like if YOU won the race, or caught a touchdown, or caught a home run ball over the fence.

We all love to get recognized. We love it when people are proud of us; when they cheer for something we've done. It feels good!

The great thing about living fully alive is that you aren't living JUST for yourself. You might enjoy getting praise from people, but you also know how to give credit to the One who makes it all possible. That's why you see some actors thank God in their award acceptance speeches . . . or why some athletes aren't afraid to say that God gave them their ability to succeed.

It all comes down to one simple idea. It's not about us. It's about Him!

PSALM 115:1 describes it this way:

> LORD, may glory be given to you, not to us.

You don't have to be a famous athlete or actor to point others to God. Anytime you use a gift God has given you, you bring glory to Him—especially when you're not afraid to say that it came from Him to begin with.

When you're elected class president, point back to God.
When you get a role in the school play, point back to God.
When you land a double full, point back to God.

When you're confident, you don't *need* to get the credit. You know others need God more than you need recognition. And you do your very best because you know that your life can point others to God. He deserves all the applause we could possibly give!

DAY 43

Your actions can point others to God.
Matthew 5:14-16

If you ever find yourself lost in a deep, dark, cave, how do you get out? Do you know? You follow the light! Because the closer you get to that light, the closer you are to finding your way out of a dark and scary situation. (There's a fun word for cave exploring, by the way: *spelunking*.)

Did you know YOU can be a light for other people? Not in the spelunking sense of the word, obviously. But you can be a *metaphorical* light. You can shine for others by showing them what a difference God is making in your life. You can show them how good has God been to you—and how living for Him is truly living to the fullest.

And when they see you—the light—they may just be able to find a way out of a dark and scary time in their lives.

Look at what Jesus said about that.

> "You are the light of the world. A town built on a hill can't be hidden. Also, people do not light a lamp and put it under a bowl. Instead, they put it on its stand. Then it gives light to everyone in the house. In the same way, let your light shine so others can see it. Then they will see the good things you do. And they will bring glory to your Father who is in heaven."
> **MATTHEW 5:14-16**

Maybe you don't always think of it this way, but people are watching the way you act. They can see that you believe in God because of the choices you make . . . the way you treat people . . . the way you have peace in difficult situations. They'll see the way you always do your best and treat others with respect. Your actions can point others to God.

When you live what you believe, you honor God . . . and you point others to Him. You shine like a light in the darkness.

Think about some ways that you can point to God with your actions.

You could invite a new kid to sit with you at lunch.
You could stand up for someone who others are making fun of.
You could do your very best on a project, even if you *could* get by with doing less.

What else could you do? Write at least one idea here and don't be afraid to let your light shine!

DAY 44

Your words can point others to God.
1 Peter 3:15

If you want to amplify God's story, a great way to do that is to use your own built-in "amplifier"—your words!

"Wow! That was the best header I've ever seen!"
"I love your sense of style."
"I can tell you worked REALLY hard on that science project. It was so cool!"

You can be an encourager. You can speak positively and build others up. You can tell people how valuable you think they are—because they're certainly valuable to God. (Everybody needs to hear more of that, don't you think?)

You can also share what you *believe* about God. It doesn't have to be weird or awkward. You can just talk about how your relationship with Him helps you in your daily life. You never know when someone might be curious about your faith, or when they might be struggling and looking for answers.

Look at what it says in 1 Peter, chapter 3:

> *Always be ready to give an answer to anyone who asks you about the hope you have. Be ready to give the reason for it. But do it gently and with respect.*
> **1 PETER 3:15**

In other words, let your actions show others the *hope* you have in God—and then be ready to talk about it and encourage them when they ask! You have hope in Jesus that will last *forever*. You know how He has completely transformed your life and brought you a new sense of purpose. You know how it feels to not just exist, but to live fully alive in Him!

So be ready to use your "microphone." Be ready to share about your faith in Jesus in case someone asks. You never know who might be ready to discover what new life in Him is all about!

Take a minute to write down a short answer to the questions on the following page so you can be ready to point others to God with your words when the time comes!

How can you be happy even when things are going wrong?

_____

_____

_____

_____

Why do you like going to church?

_____

_____

_____

Why are you nice to that kid?

_____

_____

_____

_____

DAY 45

Your story can point others to God.
2 Corinthians 12:9

Here's a timeline for you to fill in. It's your life—from the minute you were born until right here and now.

Go ahead and fill in the timeline with your life story. Definitely write in when you first decided to put your faith in Jesus. And include the other big moments that stand out to you. It could be good things, like when you moved to your new town, or when you got chosen for an award, or the first time you met your best friend. It could be difficult things, like when something happened in your family, or when you got really sick.

Take a step back and look at all that's happened so far. This is YOUR story. No one else has one just like it! And you're just getting started.

When you share your story with others, it gives them an idea of how God has worked in your life . . . the BIG ways He showed up, and the small—but still just as meaningful—ways.

_____'s AMPED Timeline

Born

There may be parts of your story that are dark or confusing. But don't try to ignore them or pretend they didn't happen, because God can use those times, too!

Paul had something to say about that in his second letter to the Corinthians. (He's talking about what God says in the first part.)

> *"My grace is all you need. My power is strongest when you are weak." So I am very happy to brag about how weak I am. Then Christ's power can rest on me.*
> **2 CORINTHIANS 12:9**

Your **whole** story can bring God glory—not just your highlight reel. When you're weak, then it shows even more clearly how strong God is, and how important He is in your life. Not only that, other people can understand what you've gone through, and how God has worked in you and changed you. **Your story can point others to God.**

Now draw a big question mark at the end of your timeline. Who knows what's coming next? **God does.** He is all you need. And He wants you to *live fully alive* as you look into your next chapter with complete confidence!

**Read my
AMPED
devotional**

AMP IT UP

Congratulations—you made it! Let's finish this with our AMPED theme song, "Fully Alive."

Listen on Spotify: http://spoti.fi/2CCLq93

Listen on YouTube: thnkor.ng/fullyalive

Let it remind you of everything we've talked about in these pages. Let it remind you to follow Jesus and stay close to Him, because He wants you to have life in the *fullest possible way.*

So, go! Live like you believe it. Turn it up . . . and live fully alive!

I see the way You live
I see the way You love
I want to live like You
I want to love the way You do

I don't want to wait, want to wait forever
I know that Your plans, that Your plans are greater
I am ready now, 'cause there's nothing better, no
And now I know

I want to live fully alive
Oh, I want to live fully alive
I want to live for You in everything I do
'Cause I want to live fully alive!